The Seventh Night

By Ladislav Mňačko

The Seventh Night

The Taste of Power

The Seventh Night

by Ladislav Mňačko

Translated from
the Slovak

Foreword by
Harry Schwartz

E. P. Dutton & Co., Inc.

New York 1969

Foreword

by Harry Schwartz

Specialist on Communist Affairs, *The New York Times*

The "Czechoslovak spring" of 1968—that brief but luminous period of an entire nation's spontaneous surge toward democracy and decency—was above all the work of that country's intellectuals. In the early and middle 1960's, the best of their reportage, fiction, movies and plays articulated their fellow citizens' deep disenchantment with the tyranny that had been imposed upon Czechoslovakia after 1948. This "revolt of the intellectuals" helped enormously to create the political situation in which it was possible for Alexander Dubček to replace Antonín Novotný. And once Dubček came to power, it was these same intellectuals who were in the forefront of the struggle for "Socialism with a soul," for a democratic, humanistic Socialism such as had never before been known in any Communist-ruled land.

Moscow recognized the key role of those who enunciated the Czechoslovak nation's deepest aspirations. No sooner had the ferment of the Dubček era begun, than the Kremlin hierarchs began insisting upon the reimposition of the tight censorship of the earlier years, demanding that the most gifted and most sensitive people in Prague and Bratislava, Brno and Košice be denied access to the printing press, the radio microphone, the television camera, the theatrical stage and other communications media. In invading Czechoslovakia, the Soviet Union and its puppets had no more urgent objective than to silence these troublesome voices so they could not spread their heretical ideas. As this is written the battle goes on, exemplified by the heroic death of Jan Palach—"Torch Number One"—whose dramatic self-sacrifice was motivated by the demand for an end to the censorship Moscow had succeeded in foisting upon occupied Czechoslovakia.

It is most fitting and important, therefore, that we should have the story of the 1968 political miracle in Czechoslovakia and the forces that brought it about as seen by one of the key intellectuals responsible for the transformation. As Ladislav Mňačko correctly points out in this fascinating volume, his name was undoubtedly included in every Soviet list of the ten Czechoslovak voices it was most important to silence by arrest or worse. He was his nation's most celebrated journalist, enjoying a prestige comparable to that of, say, James Reston or Walter Lippmann, though his writing was more often in the traditions of Richard Harding Davis and the muckraking of Upton Sinclair. The impact of his most important books on the Czechoslovak political situation was akin to that of a cross between Ilya Ehrenburg's *Memoirs* and Alexander Solzhenitsyn's *One Day in the Life of Ivan Denisovich* upon the Soviet scene. It was a major political event in 1967 when Mr. Mňačko announced from abroad that, in protest against the Prague government's pro-Arab policy in the Middle East, he would not go home, but would go to Israel instead. And it was very early in the Dubček era that a powerful and insistent demand began to be heard in Czechoslovakia that he be invited back, and that his citizenship and Communist Party membership be restored, thus undoing the punishments meted out upon him for his pro-Israeli pronouncements. He returned home, but only a few months later the Soviet Army came and he fled abroad as this book recounts.

In this volume Mr. Mňačko makes no attempt to conceal the fact that he has a many-hued past. In 1948 he was a convinced, naïve Communist who was certain his country's political transformation would bring the millennium. In the early 1950's he lent his considerable gifts to the propaganda campaign that accompanied the purges, helping to persuade an incredulous nation that innocent men were guilty. But as he matured and gained a better insight into the political realities of his homeland, he sought to atone for his past errors by helping to lead the struggle for rehabilitation of the innocent and for changing the system that had made frame-ups possible. As early as 1956 he was calling publicly for destruction of the secret police dossiers whose contents could spell the difference between life and death, freedom and prison for tens of thousands of his countrymen. Even now Mr. Mňačko still clings to his Communist ideals and he has some views on world issues that many in the West will reject. Nevertheless he was a witness—at or near the center of the political stage—for most of the past two decades in Czechoslovakia, and was one of the key figures who helped unleash the crisis of conscience that made possible the glorious and tragic events of 1968. He speaks for Free Czechoslovakia at a time when many of its other best voices are involuntarily mute.

The Seventh Night

The
First

On the night of August 20 I went to bed as usual. My life has taken many unexpected turns, and called for constant improvisation, but it has also formed certain habits, an order of its own. To eat well and eat my fill is part of it—and, above all, to sleep well and soundly; that is probably the "secret" of the strong nerves so many people envy me. To sleep well at every season of the year and—when circumstances demand it—at any time of day or night, morning or afternoon: in the heavy damp of the Vietnam jungle on matting sticky with sweat; in the surprising cold of the Sinai Desert, where my teeth would not stop chattering however I snuggled down into my sleeping bag; in the Mongolian steppes or the Siberian taiga; in the rarefied air of high mountains or the balmy air of a tropical coast; in the air-conditioned rooms of luxury hotels or bedding down in the stink of sweat and urine; near the Arctic Circle when the sun does not set, or on board a ship plowing the waves beneath the Southern Cross; on an improvised bed of pine needles in a mountain sheepfold; on a sweet-scented haystack; on a prison bunk, in a sleeping-car berth or a coach packed so tight you have to stand on one leg; in partisan mountain fastnesses on the frozen ground, in hammocks, on the bare earth; in a car roaring into the distance; shrapnel can be flying overhead, a mountain stream gurgling, the sea whispering, saxophones wailing, cicadas trilling, wild animals roaring, airplanes thundering, streetcars rattling, drunks bawling; under arc lights, in dark caves, in the irritating flicker of red neon—I can sleep, I can sleep alone or sandwiched in a narrow bed, or with an attractive woman at my side; I can sleep at any time, in any place, lying anyhow.

It is a very simple thing for me to fall asleep: I only have to close my eyes; I need no sleeping pills, no soft music, no boring book.

It is one of the constant things in my haphazard life, when I do not know where I shall be tomorrow or an hour from now, when I do not know what I shall have to eat or where I shall be able to sleep, when I do not know whether I shall be free or in prison, hungry, thirsty, or sated with my favorite delicacies, whether I shall be healthy or sick; whether I shall be alone or in company, at home, traveling, or abroad: in the roundabout of the unforeseen and unforeseeable there is one thing certain, and that is sleep; somewhere I shall fall asleep and I shall sleep, whatever happens to me or around me.

I enjoy deep, dreamless sleep. Psychiatrists say it is impossible, and that when you are asleep you are living that other life, the life of dreams, and that there are no exceptions to this rule. Maybe they are right; I can neither prove nor disprove it, for perhaps I too have dreams, perhaps I dream uninterruptedly, but if I do, I know nothing about them. My consciousness, my subconscious, my memory, records nothing of any dreams I may be having.

Yet there are times, few and far between, when I suddenly wake from profound slumber: I wake up without any obvious reason, and I hate it. My bed, always so comfortable, seems hard and lumpy, the bedclothes weigh me down; I toss and turn, force my eyes to close, afraid of the light and afraid of the darkness, afraid, afraid, drenched in sweat, I know I'll not fall asleep again till morning. This is the evil hour, the hour of shadows, and there is no refuge and no cure; it is the hour when you are alone with yourself, the hour of humiliations, doubts and shame; forgotten sins and deceits and moments of cowardice march across the bed, provoking, annoying, disturbing, growling, reproaching, threatening and laughing at you. I ought to get up and dress and go out into the deserted streets, or reach for the book on my bedside table; but I cannot bring myself to do anything; I am too weak-willed to oppose the carnival of shadows, low desires, suppressed doubts and tormenting reproaches. It is like an aching tooth; you pass your tongue over it again and again, perversely assuring yourself that it hurts, it still hurts, it's hurting like anything. . . .

Then there is instinct. In the middle of an ordinary, normal night, you suddenly feel there's something wrong. The telephone may ring in the dead of night. Your wife cannot resist the temptation to ask what you want for dinner tomorrow. An unexpected guest rings the doorbell. A mouse squeaks in a corner, a tiny little mouse you can barely hear. Isn't it strange? The street cleaners are thundering along the street in their trucks, nearby the dairyman is rolling out milk cans, drunks are bawling in thick voices, one of the neighbors setting out on a long journey tries to start a cold engine, a solitary woman hurrying home clicks along the pavement in high heels—night, and especially night in a big city, is full of sound and movement; there is always someone awake, someone getting up and someone else going to bed; the night is full of noises; it is an ordinary night when everything is normal, and yet the thin squeak of a tiny mouse is enough to wake you and you lie there sleepless, wondering if it's really only a mouse. Soon you are sure it's a mouse; but it may run over the bed you are lying on, run across your face . . . the mouse being there is wrong, it's not normal, it's as disturbing as a stranger in the place, as something extraordinary, something that is not an everyday—or rather every night —occurrence; this tiny unexpected sound disturbs your accustomed, normal, safe night's sleep and signals that there is something wrong, something is not as it should be . . . there is something wrong with you . . . with your little world. . . .

That night of the twentieth to the twenty-first of August, it was the silence that woke me. The moment I opened my eyes I knew it was not my rare evil hour; in fact it was almost too early in the night for it to be that; I was too lazy to reach for my watch, but I was sure it could not be much past midnight . . . the quiet was so unusual, so abnormal at that early hour of the night in our street that it woke me.

For a moment I wondered whether I had forgotten to open

the window. But I felt sure the window was open, and then I could see it was, for the light of the powerful streetlamps below came into the room, and unless I pulled the blinds down, which I never did, it was never quite dark.

I listened to the night. What had happened to the nightly brawlers outside the bar on the corner? Where were the long-haired hippies with the guitar and the strange, belated serenades they wailed about this time? No late footsteps, no sound of the high-heeled young woman hurrying home (I knew well enough where she had been, but it was none of my business), no cars to disturb the quiet; the city was not dead—somewhere in the distance the usual pulse of night life was beating—but here, in our street that I knew so well, that I had seen and heard so often that it was a part of me, there was something wrong. . . .

Don't be a fool, I cursed myself and turned over; I shut my eyes but still sleep did not come. Was it nerves? Were my nerves giving way? They won't last forever, they can't, and it's not so long since the night I phoned my doctor at half-past two in the morning, in a panic, to ask him what the symptoms of heart failure are. It's about the time of life for all sorts of trouble I never had before, and always laughed at in my wild youth. There would be nothing strange about it, after the physical, mental and moral ups and downs of the last few years, if my nerves . . .

Modern man, hunted as he is, longs for peace and quiet and goes to any lengths and any expense to get it, and yet it is unbelievable that this very quiet can disturb you, throb, shout, and alarm you. . . .

I got up and put my head out of the window.

The street was unusually empty. There was only one window with a light in it, the window of the bleached blonde, the amateur and not very successful prostitute who occasionally accosted passersby: "All on your own tonight, honey?" She was leaning out of her window now, the only living creature awake. The silly fool, it wasn't her night, it was a strange, unusual night. And she rarely had any luck even when it wasn't strange.

I was just going back to bed, reassured that the city was not dead, the blonde was at her post and everything was O.K., when a slight, barely recognizable change in the appearance of the house opposite caught my eye. I stiffened. It took me quite awhile to see what the change was. The dark green blind in the window facing mine, which had been down a few minutes ago, had changed its shape, was bulging out into the street, and the bulge was made by something round; it could only be a human head.

And suddenly I felt sure that from all those dark windows eyes were watching, tense, scared, wide open . . .

I no longer cursed myself for a fool; there really was something wrong; something audible and visible in that motionless silence was wrong. There was something threatening, menacing, unknown, hanging over the sleeping city of Bratislava—was it really sleeping?

The gloomy spell of the motionless night was broken by heavy, determined steps. Someone was coming down the street; I could see him, a soldier, a young soldier, probably on his way back to his barracks after seeing his girl, he'd overstayed his leave, there'd be the charge room, maybe the guardhouse . . . he came on down the street, through the beam of light from the blonde's window, and the only strange thing about it was that she didn't call out to him with the words she kept for soldiers passing by. Perhaps she wasn't feeling up to it, and anyway it was obvious the soldier had overstayed his leave and was anxious about it; he'd hardly feel in the mood for that sort of game.

The sound of the soldier's steps receded in the vague darkness of the street. For a moment, but only for a moment while they were audible, they had driven the feeling of anxiety out of my mind. The silence the soldier had broken was again menacing.

Was I suffering from hallucinations? Or was I just overwrought? (Wasn't there some connection between having hallucinations and being overwrought, anyway?) Fear of something indefinite, unknown, oppressed me. It was stronger than everything else—stronger than my nerves, than my self-ridicule, than night or day, midnight . . .

I picked up the receiver to phone Peter. The line was dead. Not a sound, not even a hum or a crackle. Out of order? That was always happening, but even when it was out of order it gave some faint sign of life. Now it was dead, deaf, dumb, just a bit of Bakelite. . . . This wasn't just menacing and strange. It was downright suspicious. . . .

I went back to the window, just in time to hear the peroxide blonde ask in a scared whisper: your phone still not working? And from the other side of the street another scared woman's voice answered: still not working. . . .

There was no doubt about it: the city was alive, the city was awake, the city was wide awake and watching; there was something going on, something unknown, menacing, something that boded ill, something I could not guess at but which could only be bad. I went up to Hannah's door on tiptoe and listened; was she asleep? Yes, I could hear her deep, regular breathing; unlike me, she slept lightly and the slightest movement, the smallest sound, would wake her.

Should I? Or shouldn't I? I turned the knob carefully, cautiously pushed the door open, cautiously and silently I went up to the bed. She moved. She woke.

"What's the matter? What's happened?"

Nothing, I reassured her, nothing. I just felt lonesome . . . I sat on the floor by her bed.

"Go back to sleep, everything's all right. Just you sleep. . . ."

I knew she wouldn't go back to sleep. I stroked her hand. I didn't want to say it but I had to.

"There's something going on . . ."

She sat up and waited to hear what was coming next.

"Something unknown, something bad. The street's deserted, as if it was dead. It's never like that. And I've got the feeling everybody's awake and they're all scared. . . ."

"Is that all? That's only your nerves, don't worry so. Go back to bed, do . . . we've got to be up early in the morning . . . go and get a bit of sleep now . . ."

The next morning, first thing, we planned to leave for Vienna. She was right, I was just being a fool. . . .

I didn't go back to bed. I went over to the window again. From the end of the street came firm, heavy steps again. Another soldier, going in the opposite direction. When he got nearer I saw it was the same one. When he reached the corner, a frightened whisper from the side street asked: "Hey, ssst! What's going on?"

"The Russians are here," he said calmly and went on. Damn fool, I wanted to yell at him, is that your idea of a joke? And sure enough, a voice came from one of the windows:

"Damn funny idea of a joke."

The soldier shrugged his shoulders and disappeared from my line of vision.

Damn fool . . . the Russians . . . impossible, out of the question, absurd . . .

Still, I went back to Hannah again.

"Some damn fool of a soldier went past and said the Russians were here. . . ."

Her reaction was the same as mine: It's absurd, out of the question, impossible . . .

Russians or no Russians, there was something in the air.

There was definitely something in the air, something heavy, cumbersome, noisy, rattling. At first it was only a vague noise, then it came nearer and turned into the noise of a plane, a strange old-fashioned rattling affair; nowadays planes sound quite different. It wasn't a passenger plane, and it wouldn't be a military plane either; there are better machines these days, and this sounded like something from before the war, but what could it possibly be doing over the city at this hour of the night? A private plane? There weren't any; some of the firms had planes, but they wouldn't be over the city at night. Where could the plane be from? From abroad? From Austria? The Austrian frontier was near enough, maybe some sporting pilot had lost his way . . . that would be it.

The noise was quite near and quite low. I hurried to the window and looked out in time to see an antediluvian monster which was not an antediluvian monster but a clumsy helicopter.

"It's a helicopter. . . ." I told Hannah.

A helicopter . . . what was a helicopter doing over the city at night? Well, whatever it was doing there, it was one of ours, because no foreign helicopter, not even a Soviet machine, could hover over the city at night like that without being forced to land by our own crews. . . .

There had been the shock of the maneuvers. Those unfortunate military maneuvers the government had announced for that week, to be held in Western Bohemia. I didn't trust those maneuvers, I didn't like the sound of them; at a time of tension like the one we were going through, the government ought not to allow any large concentration of forces; there's no trusting brass hats, it was a general—General Kodaj—whose speech in the National Assembly had brought on a grave political crisis; we'd already had one threat of a military putsch; you could never guess what game the military were up to, and they could plot happily away under the cloak of military secrecy; in every state the army is a power unto itself. Only a few days earlier, reading about the maneuvers they were preparing, I had said to Hannah: "I don't like the look of it, it can start something bad, something that can't be undone."

The helicopter circled the city, and again, and again; we listened to the noise it was making, silent, but watchful.

When it started its fifth circle, I told Hannah to get dressed. "Come on, let's dress and go out; there's something bad going on, I'm sure of it now, something bad; we might not know anything about it out in this isolated neighborhood, but if we walk around the streets a little . . ."

We went out. Our street was quiet and deserted and there was nothing to suggest that my fears were justified: there were no terrified eyes watching from behind the drawn curtains, everything was just as it ought to be, and the fact that there was not a soul about seemed just a coincidence.

There was, though; in fact there were a lot of them, coming around the corner; a gang of excited hippies burst into the quiet street, singing and shouting, just for the hell of it, singing the "International."

There were about thirty of them, and they took no notice of

us as they crowded past, singing the "International" and waking
the sleepers with their shouting and bellowing. Not long afterward, we met another gang near the square. The Russians . . .
maneuvers . . . it was only the hippies who'd decided to make
whoopee in the city, that was what all the tension and fear had
grown out of. . . .

We crossed Suché Mýto. It was all quiet there, nobody and
nothing unusual.

Nothing unusual? What were those vague shadowy shapes
standing in line all along Stefanik Street? Trucks? They couldn't
be trucks because the road was closed for repairs; nothing could
be driven along it. . . .

Then we were sure. Tanks. Tanks can drive along a street
that is torn up for repairs. Tanks can drive anywhere.

Tanks. A lot of tanks. Standing at regular intervals, engines
switched off. Each was painted right down the center with a
broad white line.

There they were, as far as we could see in that light. Great
tanks with menacing guns, armored cars with machine gunners
holding their weapons at the ready, trucks packed with armed
infantry.

We walked down a street leading to the Danube. On what
used to be called Stalin Square—*used* to be?—was a solitary
tank with a damaged caterpillar track. The hippies we had
passed earlier, in such high spirits, were engaged in an unequal
struggle with the monster. They were throwing cobblestones at
the thick shot-proof steel sides, trying to break it up with park
benches. The gunners had not closed the turret but were standing there helplessly with their fingers on their triggers, or using
the butts of their rifles to keep the invading youngsters off the
tank. A salvo of machine-gun fire cut through the night. As
though it was a prearranged signal, guns spoke from all over
the city. They stopped as suddenly as they had begun. I dragged
Hannah after me into a side street. For the time being they were
firing into the air, but before long it might not be into the air.
The hippies were still trying to get that tank—our useless,
cynical, noncommitted young people. . . . In the days to come

they would be in the forefront of the passive resistance to the flood of steel, and more than one of them would pay for it with his life. . . .

We passed the broadcasting station, the Post Office, the Town Hall. It was the same thing everywhere: a few tanks with their guns pointing in all directions, ready to shoot up the town at the slightest sign of armed resistance. In front of the Reduta, on the riverbank, an armored car was surrounded by dozens of young people in lively discussion with the crew. An officer drove up in a jeep and ordered them to disperse; his voice was arrogant, domineering and cruel. They did not disperse. He ordered the men to fire a warning shot. They still did not disperse. The officer went away with a gesture of helpless fury.

We walked along the river; the embankment was crowded and the one bridge over the Danube was full of tanks, too, standing one behind the other. On the other side of the river, past the Castle, rolled another column of the steel monsters.

They had come. Some years ago one of my friends, the Czech writer Jariš, published a book entitled *They Will Come,* describing all the hopes and longings, all the impatience with which we had waited for them to come, then; they came, and fulfilled the hopes we had placed in them.

Now they had come for the second time. Nobody had been waiting for them. Everyone was afraid of their coming. Nobody believed they really would come. But they had come. There they were. The Russians had come.

One of the hopes of one small section of humanity was living its last hours. One illusion of freedom was dying. The Russians had come. The Russians were there. Deep in his heart everyone had rather feared they might come, but nobody wanted to admit it. We did all we could to convince one another that it was impossible, out of the question, absurd, stupid, something they could not afford to risk, something they would not dare to do, they would not do such a thing, they were not like that, now.

We met some friends walking along the embankment; they had the Russians right under their windows. They had also been able to hear the news on the radio before it went off the air, and had telephoned friends before the phones went dead. They heard a special news broadcast from Vienna: At eleven-thirty the armies of five members of the Warsaw Pact crossed the Czechoslovak frontier all along its length, from the friendly territory of neighboring Socialist states. In a few hours they had occupied Prague, Bratislava, Ostrava and Brno. They were now completing the occupation of the country, making for Pilsen and České Budějovice. They occupied the offices of the central secretariat of the Communist Party of Czechoslovakia, while a meeting of the Executive Committee was in progress. They interned Alexander Dubček, Oldřich Černík, Josef Smrkovský and Čestmir Čísař and took them off to an unknown destination. Next morning we should be told that they had been "invited" by honorable Communists to come and prevent the counterrevolution from getting the upper hand; next morning they would announce the formation of a new government, with the names of the ministers. I could have named the ministers in advance, myself, and there was not much risk I'd be wrong.

That was what occurred to me, in the small hours of that night, as I stood on the bank of the Danube and watched the menacing steel monsters rolling through the streets of the city. There was no hitch in the military operations, the invaders met with no resistance, and each unit knew exactly how far to go and where to stop. Since there was no opposition it was not an easy matter; the movements of five armies had to be coordinated, they had to be prevented from attacking each other in the darkness; to make recognition easy they had painted those broad white lines down their vehicles of destruction; they had to keep to the direction laid down beforehand and they had to know in advance where the important government buildings were, the post offices and banks, the radio and television broadcasting stations, the newspaper offices and the telephone exchanges. They had to find all this out from maps of our towns, and they had to find the towns themselves; the invasion took us completely by surprise, the occupation was upon us before the most essential defensive measures could be taken. No resistance was possible, for our strategy did not take into account the possibility of attack from the side it eventually came from. During those weeks of tension, I had nourished a tiny flicker of hope that in political and military circles people had considered the possibility and taken the minimum of preparatory steps; watching the concentration of power pouring over that one bridge, and imagining the same thing going on over all our bridges, along all our roads, across all our frontier posts, right along those twelve hundred some miles of common frontier, and remembering how their technique had enabled them to divide our country into so many separate zones, I was forced to laugh at my own naïve little flicker of hope. It was a very well-prepared operation, probably planned long before; if they planned so thoroughly along military lines, they had probably thought the rest out, too. We were in a tough spot, and we would be for a long time yet, for long decades, perhaps up to the last world war of all, with its problematical promise of "liberation," the liberation of the land from every living thing.

That was what occurred to me that night, and there were few who viewed the arrival of the Russians in any other light; at that moment, watching the never-ending stream of steel monsters, few could have thought that anything could yet be done, that everything was not yet lost, that in fact nothing was yet lost, that the world would witness such a surprise as it had never yet seen, that the cruel weeks of occupation would surpass the excitement of the "Prague spring" and the Czechoslovakia "hot summer." That Czechoslovakia would stand up to the terrific strain, that the country would stand up to it in spite of twenty tank divisions, that the country would hold out until the faithless aggressor was recognized and condemned by the whole of the civilized world. That brute physical force, cynical and armored in manganese steel to boot, was not the only driving force in history, and that there was another force, that of the weak and helpless and unarmed, a force that no steel could deal with. . . .

I knew nothing of that as I stood there on the embankment in Bratislava, at the hour when night turns into morning. Who knew it that night? Alexander Dubček, carted off "to an unknown destination"? Millions of sleepers knew nothing about the whole business, as yet. What would they do when they awoke to this?

A few days later journalists would be writing about the miracle, about the amazing moral victory, the invincible free will and unity of these two nations in their common state, about their unparalleled political and moral strength. But there was nothing of this to be heard or seen yet. All that could be seen were the tanks, tanks, tanks and more tanks, and two little figures coming toward us along the embankment, two civilians weaving this way and that and propping each other up; they'd probably been thrown out of some nightclub or other. Laughing themselves sick as they staggered past the tanks, one said to the other: "Maneuvers, that's what it is, you damn fool; didn't you read in the papers about the new maneuvers?"

I looked more closely at the speaker. It seemed to me that this was Josef Schweik himself. He had come out into the streets.

Czechoslovakia has been occupied, ravished, held tight in the clutches of her five closest, most loyal and ardent friends and allies. From the military point of view it may have been a brilliant operation; some of those who inspired it may yet believe they have struck a powerful blow at the enemies of peace and Socialism. But they can have and will have no joy from this victory. With the aid of her potential enemies, the Soviet Union has killed the only sincere friendship she enjoyed. The Soviet Union is hated in Hungary, in Poland, in Ulbricht's East Germany; as soon as they can they will rise against her; it will happen, and it is going to happen, at a time when it will make things hard for Moscow. Our country would have stood by her through thick and thin, we would not have betrayed her as the "faithful" will.

Standing there alone and looking into the muddy waters of the Danube, it is hard to know whether to be sad or relieved. This is the hour of truth. That is a good thing. . . .

That is a good thing, I repeated to myself at the hour when night turns into morning.

And something else.

It serves us right. . . .

And something else. . . . .
It serves me right. . . .

I stood there alone for a long time. Hannah had gone over to
see some friends to find out more. The Russians had come, and
that forced everyone to face new problems that had not even
been posed the day before. The Russians had come, and it
would be foolish to pretend they had come for other reasons
than the real one. We could expect them to set up a new government that very morning; we knew what sort of a government
it would be, and we could tell what their first moves would be.
The friend we had run into an hour earlier made no secret of
what h⌄ thought about it all—and about me.

"You ought to get away. There's still time. . . ."

He was thinking of the same thing as I was. In the list of
vermin to be shot, my name would be among the first ten. There
would be a reign of terror, discrimination, trials, sentences
passed. There would be more than that; there would be "Soviet
interests," including their interest in certain individuals. I would
probably belong to those so honored. A short stint in Siberia
. . . I've been there and I like singing Leshchenko's song:

A ya Sibiryi, Sibiryi neboyusya . . .

It's a fine song, as long as you're singing it over a bottle of
vodka, somewhere safe and comfortable. Run away? No, not
yet. I want to see what happens. I want to be able to remember
it. I want to be witness and judge and prosecution. Hannah is a
more practical-minded creature and thinks of the "less important" things as well. To stay in the country, that's right, but
where are you going to sleep? Not at home . . . The friends
she had gone to look up were the sort who do not let you down
in the moment of need.

I stood there alone for a long, long time, saying over and
over again: serves us right, serves me right. . . . I felt resigned.
Not confused or unclear. I had settled all that a bit sooner than
others who still would have to work it out. The pitiless inner
struggle between the strictly logical view of the facts and the

sentimental discipline of a Communist had already been fought out in my mind. I had proved it to myself, my friends, the Party, the world, a year earlier when I went to Israel. . . .

Israel. . . . I had seen Soviet tanks in the Sinai Desert, too. Hundreds of Soviet tanks, worthless scrap that the sand will bury in time, for it would not be worth the expense to move them to a more civilized spot. The tanks I was watching now were not scrap. But they were the same tanks, and had come with the same end in view. In the interest of "higher interests," they were out to strangle the freedom of a small, helpless nation. Then, there were some who did not understand my attitude, but now, in a day or two, I would be hearing from a disheartened, dejected fellow writer, one of the sharpest critics of what had then seemed rather incomprehensible on my part: Latzo, now I know what an aggressor is.

I don't feel like saying "I told you so." I would rather he didn't know what it was, I'd rather nobody ever had to know. . . . But every "I'd rather" is a lament, a vain lament for something that was dear to us and has been smashed. . . .

I was quite clear, that dawn, about what had happened and what it was going to mean, but over and over again I asked myself: Where, when, at what moment, in which fateful second of our history did we make the false step that brought us to this? The fact that the Russians had come was not only the ultimate result of their own unforgivable error, but it also was somewhere in us, in our own actions, it was our error, too, our wrong assessment of our own ability, our own reality. And when should I work it out, if not in this hour of truth? The time to free myself of all false sentiment, illusion, self-deception. Now when the hour of truth had come to us in this cruel and brutal shape, should we dress her up in the Emperor's nonexistent clothes? Let others do that. We cannot afford the luxury of destroying ourselves. Only the naked truth, however bitter and unpalatable, can liberate and redeem.

Where was our fateful error? When was it that in us, in me, a once noble idea began to degenerate? At which moment did we betray ourselves, when did we break faith and founder between Scylla and Charybdis?

The salient points are not few; they are marked by the significant points in our history: 1938, Munich; 1945, liberation; 1948, February; 1956, the Twentieth Congress of the Communist Party of the Soviet Union; 1964, the open fight for democratization begins; 1968, Dubček leads the Party. Where, when, which year? Or was it all the time, every year?

1938—our fate was decided behind our backs.

1945—victory over Fascism. The Red Army liberated our country.

1948—final and definite victory of the working class.

1956—the end of Stalinism.

1964—rehabilitation of the humanist ideals of Communism.

1968—victory of democracy over the dictatorship of a bureaucratic administrative system.

Were we not deceiving ourselves, while in fact things were very different?

The history of postwar Czechoslovakia cannot be considered apart from what happened at Munich. The Munich agreement on Czechoslovakia was an eloquent example of the fate of small nations who rely on "great allies" and protectors. The countries that had stood at the cradle of the Czechoslovak Republic, responsible in a way for "creating" it, and that had guaranteed our independence and security, decided at Munich that this Republic should be destroyed and the two small nations it comprised should be enslaved and perhaps liquidated. Umbrella Chamberlain referred to the affair with unconcealed, cynical brutality: Great Britain was not going to fight for a country she knew nothing about. . . . When the fate of Czechoslovakia was being decided in Munich, the Czechoslovak representative was not even admitted to the negotiations.

(We shall have to get used to this feature of our history. In Warsaw in the summer of 1968, when five Socialist countries met to decide the fate of Czechoslovakia, it was once again in the absence of our representatives.)

Perhaps it will not be out of place here to recall the direct connection between the fact that Great Britain and France lost their position as Great Powers, and the signing of the Munich agreement by these two countries. The Czechoslovak people drew clear conclusions from it. We are a small country and we cannot stand alone in the heart of restless and disturbed Europe; we must follow a different policy, and rely on those international forces that are capable of fulfilling their obligations. The enslaved, oppressed people of Czechoslovakia turned their hopeful eyes in one direction only. They will come, they will save us from annihilation, and with them at our side we need have no fears. They will come, naturally, as the representatives of a Socialist country, and they will expect something from us in return for liberating us—but the whole nation agreed with this at the time. Before the war Czechoslovakia had already been ripening for revolutionary social change.

Today these hopes, too, leave a bad taste in the mouth. The small nation searches in vain for permanent guarantees of its independence and its freedom. It is and clearly always will be a pawn in the game played by the Great Powers, even more so in this cynical century which has devaluated all values.

The profound and unresolved crisis of Europe was revealed in all its nakedness at Munich.

All that remained to the Czech and Slovak peoples was the bitter reproach: the great of this world decided our fate behind our backs.

Is this really the truth? And if it is, is it the whole truth? The Great Powers decided our fate behind our backs, but it was primarily our own existence that was at stake. Apart from the alibi "behind our backs," the final decision was one that we ourselves had to take. The question before us was no different from the one that faced almost all the small nations of Europe before long.

We had not the slightest hope of standing up to Hitler's enormous striking force, but had the Poles or the Danes any greater hope, the Norwegians, the Dutch, the Belgians, the Yugoslavs, the Greeks, or—even—the Albanians? Had the Romanians, the Finns or the Hungarians any greater hope? I do not know how great the will to resist was in any of these peoples, but in Czechoslovakia, in spite of the decision of the Great Powers and in spite of our betrayal by our allies, the will to resist was complete and intact.

The real truth is that it was not only our allies who betrayed us. The legend of "behind our backs" is only a legend serving to cover up our own helplessness, our own capitulation. We, too, failed at the decisive moment; we, too, betrayed our own cause.

I do not know how long we might have been able to hold out from the military point of view. Probably not for long. But after the war we would have been a nation conscious that it had done all in its power to preserve its own existence, and victory would not have had that bitter flavor to it. . . .

We had an excellently equipped army then; it surrendered the country to the invaders without offering any resistance. Years later this was to happen again. We would have an excellently equipped army which cost us fantastic sums to maintain; its mobility and excessive numbers would be one of the causes of our economic troubles; the budget allotments for military expenditure would strain the whole economy of the country to the limits of its capacity. This trained and equipped army, for the second time, would surrender the country to the invaders. Is not every such appeal to force of only temporary validity in spite of the aggressor's intention to settle a crisis by brute force and impose a final solution once and for all? Can it be assumed that the occupation of Czechoslovakia makes the loss of its independence final? A highly topical question today is: when we are again a free and independent state, shall we again have a well-trained, well-equipped, expensive army? Shall we spend all those billions every year to equip it even more effectively, to have it even better prepared for battle? Is this not a useless luxury for a country like Czechoslovakia? In the present European context, would Czechoslovakia be able to defend and hold its far from simple frontiers? The armies of the five Socialist states had divided Czechoslovakia neatly into ten zones before the Czechoslovak High Command even realized the changed state of affairs. In 1938 Czechoslovakia was almost hermetically surrounded by enemy states; it was not only Germany, but also Hungary and Poland, that shared in the partition of Czechoslovakia. Thirty years later Czechoslovakia was almost hermetically surrounded by the Warsaw Pact states. It is and will remain a cruel irony that all the defensive efforts of Czechoslovakia were directed toward frontiers from which, in the hour of greatest need, there was no threat, and from which no danger came. It was on the Bavarian frontier that the greatest concentration of Czechoslovak troops was to be found, units having been transferred there from other parts of the country. Even if the will to resist had existed, resistance in that area was superfluous. The High Command of the five occupation armies in all probability appreciated this situation. The serious suspicion arises whether the "autumn maneuvers" on the Bavarian frontier were not directly inspired by Moscow to ensure the smooth course of the occupation itself.

They need have had no fear. The Czechoslovak Government did not, in the few hours of freedom of decision left to it, declare the rapidly proceeding occupation of the country to be an act of military aggression; they did not announce that the country was in a state of war with the five Socialist countries which in the most brutal fashion had infringed and trampled underfoot the sovereignty of Czechoslovakia and the inviolability of her frontiers, solemnly guaranteed by those very powers. If they had, the position of Czechoslovakia in international law would be clearer and better defined today.

This is not to be taken as reproaching the President or Dubček. In those hours of crisis they acted like men of courage, and they still act so today; they are wise statesmen, equal to the tasks imposed on them and the opportunities offered. They are still living and acting in the hope that this criminal misunderstanding will be cleared up, that something may still be saved from the wreck. I believe this is a vain hope. Nothing can be expected of allies who disregarded their solemn obligations in such a cynical, brutal, barbarian way, allies who tore their international agreements up as Hitler did, agreements they themselves had inspired; there can be no trusting in their promises, in any agreement reached, any assurances given. The Czechoslovak people have been cured for good of all illusions about friendship and alliance with the Soviet Union as the guarantee of Czechoslovak sovereignty and security. That—maybe—is a positive side to the barbarous occupation of the country. Not long ago we relied on others, but today we know that we are alone, that we shall always be alone, and that we cannot expect decent treatment from either the East or the West; the nineteenth-century poet's words fit us well enough:

> "Trust no one in the wide, wide world;
> We have no friends out there . . ."

This experience has cost us dear, and will still have to be paid for. The consciousness of nations grows in proportion to their ability to get rid of false legends and illusions. The highest quality of mankind, and of every nation, is the ability to recognize limits and opportunities. However cruel the reality may be, to recognize it for what it is becomes a positive factor in shaping our own destiny.

Czechoslovakia is a small country, and in her short history all her friends and allies have betrayed her.

The present occupation of Czechoslovakia can be explained only, or rather primarily, by what happened to our peoples at the time of the Munich betrayal. . . .

What really happened as the result of this agreement, and around it, has never been fully revealed to the Czechoslovak people, even today. They have not been allowed to know. They were never supposed to find out. Munich was and still is taboo for Czechoslovak historians, journalists, writers. It is worth noting how very few honest works on this exciting subject have been written in Czechoslovakia since the war, even if numerous timid attempts at analysis, incomplete and biased, set out to prove that:

Our fate was decided at Munich behind our backs.

Munich was a dirty game played by world imperialism.

Our betrayal by our allies was capped by the treachery of the Czechoslovak bourgeoisie, surrendering the Republic without a struggle for fear that once in arms the people would become too radical and would transform the fight for national freedom into a Socialist revolution. (There were such revolutionary tendencies in Czechoslovakia at the time.)

The Communists represented the only political party, the only political force to fight against capitulation and to call the nation to fight for its freedom and to oppose the mortal threat of Fascism. . . .

The Czechoslovak President, Eduard Beneš, played an active part in preparing the capitulation. At the decisive moment his political conception of the state failed. . . .

The citizen who tries to find an explanation can learn all this from the fairly extensive literature about Munich. Any attempt, however timid, to look at this crucial point in Czechoslovak history from another angle, was very sharply suppressed.

For twenty years the Czechoslovaks have been told the legend of the loyal Soviet alliance, of the Soviet Union as the only ally willing to stand by its treaty obligations. This legend is based on the official protests lodged by the Soviet Government against the Munich agreement and the occupation of Czechoslovakia. It is hard, today, to judge the value of something that never happened. The Soviet Union did not at that time give us any military aid, for the simple reason that our government did not ask for it, and for the more cogent reason that the Soviet Union was not in a position to give any effective aid. The Soviet Union had no common frontier either with Czechoslovakia or with Germany as things then stood. In such circumstances solemn declarations of that sort are no more valuable than the solemn declarations made by China today about the help she will give Albania. And finally, the treaty by which the Soviet Union bound itself to give military aid to Czechoslovakia was not a bilateral one, but was subject to active military aid being given by France. Only if France entered a war on behalf of Czechoslovakia was the Soviet Union in duty bound to give military aid as well. Soviet politicians explained their "non-aid" to menaced Czechoslovakia as the consequence of the nonfulfillment of these complicated treaty obligations. They would have liked to, but France did not want to, and thus the treaty was not valid. . . .

I do not think that the Soviet Union could have given us any very effective aid, nor is it certain that she would have been willing to even if Czechoslovakia had asked for it. "If only" is a phrase that has no validity in the writing of history, and is always suspect.

If that is how things were, it should be said so openly and honestly. And—from the Communist point of view—it is wrong to falsify history and touch it up, to blame everybody else and not to mention one's own share of the blame for what happened.

Munich was not only the failure of Eduard Beneš and the betrayal of the country by the bourgeoisie.

It is true that Beneš let us down, that he failed his people. Beneš was an unlucky failure as a politician, and would fail them again in the revolutionary year of 1948, disappointing the hopes of his loyal supporters who expected him to be a man of action.

But it was not only Beneš who failed us in the days of Munich; the leader of the Communist Party, Klement Gottwald, failed us too, all along the line. From him, above all from him, and in the last hours before the capitulation, from him alone, the whole nation expected the decisive, liberating, fateful word: Fight! We're going to fight! We're going to act! A hundred thousand people listening attentively, with enthusiastic agreement, heard Gottwald say that we would never capitulate, but it was an empty phrase. He was not the only one to fear decisive responsibility at that decisive moment. Instead of issuing a clear call that would have had the support of the whole people, in those days when all was not yet lost, he began preparing for the Party to go underground. He was probably already considering his own emigration to Moscow. Of course we could not have held out. But after the defeat of Fascism, Czechoslovakia would have had a seat at the victors' table in other circumstances and not in the role of a suppliant.

The question whether we should or should not have fought then is still not clear to the people of Czechoslovakia. The opponents of active military opposition say they would have made mincemeat of us. . . . But what else did they do, and what else did they intend to do? Three hundred and fifty thousand tortured and beaten to death or executed, even if it includes the tragic fate of the seventy-seven thousand Czech Jews, was a heavy price to be paid by a nation that did not fight, that gave way before the threat of force, and over whose territory no major operations and battles were fought. Were it not for the victory won by others, and primarily by the Red Army, there would hardly be any Czech nation at all today, and Slovakia would probably be a national park for the tourists of Greater Germany, where they might still be able to see the strange habits of the last remnants of the inferior Slav race. . . . Disregarding the Slovak National Rising, Czechoslovakia did nothing significant to further her own liberation, except for the political campaigns undertaken in exile; her active share in the defeat of Nazism was the minimum.

The failure of Gottwald, the failure of the Communist Party during the fateful days of Munich, had fateful consequences for the postwar setup in Czechoslovakia and for the policy of the Party. We were under too heavy an obligation to the Soviet liberators of our country. Stalin's works were published in enormous editions, touched up to suit the fashion of the day. The informed student looked in vain in the speeches of 1938 for the sharp criticism Stalin hurled in Gottwald's face. Gottwald had only Stalin's inconsistency, or his generosity, to thank that he was alive at all. The "mercy" with which he was favored by the otherwise inexorable Stalin became Gottwald's lifelong obligation and the debt he had to repay. Gottwald just was not Tito. He was not the popular leader steeled in the fight. He returned to rule as an *émigré,* and probably with the check for his life in exile still unpaid. The hopes of the Party and of the people would be placed in him, but he would fail them, he would fail at every decisive moment; he would fail in 1945, wrongly assessing the real situation in the country; he would fail in 1948 and he would fail in the period of the trials, handing over to the executioner his intimate friends and those he had worked with for many long years—even if it cost him a great effort. Acts which were going to appear to be the results of his own will, were not. He was only carrying out orders from Stalin.

At the fateful crossroads of history, the Czech and Slovak nations living together in one state were to be fought over by two ancient rivals, contending for the dominating influence in the little country; both rivals were to reveal themselves politically as well as morally bankrupt. Their "historical account" would be settled at the expense of the sufferings and national pride of the whole nation. Were it not for the capitulation in the face of Munich, Stalin could not in Yalta have made such a self-assured demand for Czechoslovakia to be included in his "sphere of interest." Stalin had the right to "claim for himself" the major influence in the lands of Hitler's defeated allies, in east and southeast Europe: Hungary, Romania and Bulgaria. The case of Yugoslavia, however, shows where his hold ended and when the limits of his partners' concessions were reached. Stalin was forced to look on when Churchill, even before the war was over, brutally suppressed the revolutionary Greek resistance movement. In the case of "renegade Yugoslavia," Stalin had to be content with the disgusting lies of a propaganda campaign. He was unable to take military action in the face of the "Yugoslav betrayal." Tito could take liberties which were denied to Gottwald. He could tell Stalin to his face: I disagree with you, Comrade Stalin! He was the beloved victor, he was an equal partner; he owed Stalin nothing—indeed it was almost the other way around.

Czechoslovakia's place at the victory table was unequal, unstable and even problematical. Stalin had to close his eyes to the obvious fact that the Slovak clerico-Fascist state had been the ally of Hitler's Germany. To the fact that the Slovak Army, too, had taken part in the invasion of the Soviet Union and that some units of the Slovak Army had even taken part in the massacre of civilians in the Ukraine. It must have been clear to every thinking observer that the price Czechoslovakia would have to pay for this "generosity" would be high indeed.

Soviet soldiers would be putting it to the Czechoslovak people less than a quarter of a century later: to despairing questions about why they had come, why they were occupying our country, they answered: our fathers liberated this country, so it's ours. . . .

At the time of Munich, Gottwald could have drawn to himself the entire state power and the undivided sympathy of the whole nation, if only he had said the decisive word, which perhaps he flinched from at the last moment. But since the study of history teaches us that nothing in politics is clear, simple and obvious, we are forced to consider whether it was he himself, on his own initiative, who flinched, or was it others who flinched and told him to act so? Could it not have been those who criticized him for it so sharply so soon afterward? It can hardly be assumed that Gottwald, the consistent internationalist, the obedient executive of the supreme international Communist organ, the Third International, acted without first consulting this supreme authority over all authorities; to put it more clearly: that he would have decided without consulting Moscow, whose word was decisive in the Third International, who had in fact created the organization in order to break through the almost complete isolation of the Soviet Union from the rest of the world.

I myself can give palpable evidence of the taboo on the Communist attitude to Munich. On the occasion of the twenty-fifth anniversary of the Munich agreement, I was asked by the editor of one of the big illustrated weeklies in Prague to write an article that would throw new light on Munich and help to explain it to the youngsters who had not lived through it and could not understand the significance of the whole episode.

"I'll write it for you, why not?" I agreed. "But you know what I'm like and you can guess how I'm likely to write about it.'

They knew, of course they knew, and that was precisely why they wanted me to do it.

I wrote the article in the form of a conversation and called it an unpleasant conversation between a fifty-year-old and a twenty-year-old about Munich. It was not long, about eight pages of typescript, but I had got into it the whole moral problem of our Czechoslovak attitude to Munich.

"Why didn't you fight, Dad?" asks the twenty-year-old son at the beginning, and is not satisfied by a single one of the arguments his father puts forward. With unrelenting impatience he asks over and over again: it was your lives at stake, why didn't you fight? I'm not asking whether your allies let you down, I'm asking why you didn't fight. I don't care whether the Czechoslovak bourgeoisie betrayed you or not, you were a Communist —why didn't you fight? The point isn't whether you could have held out or not; there are other nations that went into battle without much hope of holding out—why didn't you fight? Geographical conditions couldn't have been so important; the Slovaks held out for two months during the Rising, far worse equipped than you were then, in the mountains, and in much worse conditions than you had—why didn't you fight?

The final answer is a box on the ears and a reproachful: "Why do you keep on at me, you bloodsucker?"

The editor was delighted with it. The chief editor was delighted. At last a breath of fresh air, even if only in small measure. That's the right way to get through to the young people; you've got to talk openly about things.

Of course it was never printed. I did not expect it would be, and not without malice I phoned the editor. They had not printed it. They couldn't. They weren't allowed to. I might as well know they'd had the chief editor up and hauled him over the coals, he'd caught it hot from the Party authorities.

From time to time editorial offices would ask whether I hadn't got something I could let them have. I had. I had an article about Munich. I would offer it, and they'd be delighted. The chief editor who had originally commissioned me to write the article got away with being "hauled over the coals." Two more who wanted to publish it did not get off so lightly. They were thrown out on their necks for their audacity. What was so dangerous and wicked about my article? It was "not Marxist." That was the way, for years and years, that the Party bureaucracy stamped out any attempt to find out even part of the truth, and not only the truth about Munich. . . .

It is not difficult to guess why this desperate "fight against

Munich" was carried on so relentlessly for years. Sufficient reason in itself was the attempt to assign the share of the blame for capitulation that could be laid at the Party's door, but this was not the only reason. Revelations in this quarter would have led straight to another question: the truth about the Fifth Party Congress at which Gottwald and his "lads from Karlín" got control of the Party leadership.

In recent years some historians, particularly younger scholars, have tried at least to raise these questions. They provoked immediate and intense disapproval from Novotný and increased "vigilance" from the censors.

Munich resulted in a profound demoralization in the two nations of Czechoslovakia. For a time the Slovak clerico-Fascists won over the great majority of the Slovak people to their separatist policy. In the fateful days of March, 1939, the Slovak Popular Party helped Hitler to destroy the remnant of Czechoslovakia. As reward they received the "Slovak State." Hitler occupied the Czech part of the country directly, through the Protectorate of Bohemia and Moravia he set up. From the very first day the Nazi occupation forces let loose a reign of terror. The Czechs replied with passive resistance, retiring into spiritual exile, turning in on themselves. Six years of this reign of terror wrought tremendous damage to the national character, demoralized the nation, but it also taught the people to adapt themselves to conditions in a ravished country. The Czechs lost their national pride for a long time to come. For years after the liberation they "envied" the Slovaks the National Rising, while the Slovaks made no secret of their ridicule of the Czechs for their "Prague revolution."

The occupation also revealed the strong side of the Czech national character. This was the only country occupied by the Germans where in spite of constant attempts they never succeeded in starting a serious Fascist movement. Czech democratic feeling was a strong enough defense against the brown plague. The Germans did not succeed in organizing even one symbolic regiment in Bohemia which could be put into the fight against Bolshevism, however hard they tried. Those who were prepared to collaborate with the occupation forces for personal gain were aware that they were cutting themselves off from their own people forever.

But the reign of terror during the Nazi occupation also fostered in the Czech character traits that immediately came to the fore at the first hint of another reign of terror—that of Stalinism. Terror, wherever it reigns, has certain permanent features: a secret police force arresting, torturing, threatening, spying and informing; a shameful justiciary, condemning innocent people to long terms of imprisonment and even to death; a harsh censorship throttling the freedom of the press; the dictatorship of one individual, of a group of individuals, or of an anonymous apparatus—their truth is the only truth, their law is the only law. After 1948, when the first signs appeared of a terror with which the Czechs already had had such intimate experience, they had no difficulty in remembering what life had been like under an earlier reign of terror, and in accommodating themselves to this new wave of terror in the way which had proved so successful with the Nazis: apparently agreeing with it all, but in fact quietly sabotaging and ridiculing it, "playing Schweik." It seems easy to govern and direct a nation like this, that offers no visible opposition and neither revolts nor protests; but it only seems so. Unfortunately one consequence of this inner exile was the absolute stagnation of economic life; individual initiative dropped to naught; it was a united front of resistance which no terror could break through. The Czechs were very conscious of this trait in their character, its advantages and disadvantages, and often discussed it, particularly with Slovaks; but it took them much longer than the Slovaks to organize active resistance. The Stalinist reign of terror was much more cruel and barbarous in Slovakia, but it never succeeded in "pacifying" the nation to the degree achieved in Bohemia and Moravia. When the Slovak intellectuals began their struggle against this terror, a struggle that involved their very existence, their calls for cooperation from their Czech colleagues went out in vain; they found no response, and they were given no more effective help than a slap on the shoulders; for years they seemed to be engaged in their hopeless struggle alone. To remind the Czechs of the cause and origin of their long-drawn-out moral crisis meant urging them to resolve it, and that meant rebellion against the terror. It took them a long time before they reached that point, but when they did the result was a movement whose forms and aims went far beyond those of the Slovak intellectuals' lonely struggle. And the beginning and the cause of the national demoralization of the Czechs was the Munich capitulation. . . .

The
Second

All day long I wandered about the town. Morning is a better counselor, as the Slovak proverb says. New units were still pouring over the Danube bridge. In those few hours the occupation had paralyzed the normal life of the country. Telephones were dead, railway traffic at a standstill, and long lines in front of bakers' shops were waiting for the bread that did not come. There was a run on the shops as people laid in supplies. But from the early hours of the morning, the radio had been broadcasting—instead of calls by a new government, and announcements of orders issued and measures taken—pleas for unity and resistance; they called what had happened by its real name: occupation, rape, aggression, the infringement of valid treaties, betrayal by our allies, unheard-of criminal barbarity.

I phoned the broadcasting studios; that morning the occupation army had allowed the telephone exchanges to function again, for there was no longer any need for secrecy—the whole territory of Czechoslovakia had been occupied by then. The invaders had interrupted passenger traffic between Prague and Bratislava; all the airfields were in their hands and they had grounded all planes on international and inland routes. International and local express trains could not run. They seem to have planned this for the first phase, before the Czech and Slovak peoples would start embracing their liberators and cheering them on, before the gates of the big factories opened to spew forth processions of workers carrying red banners, before the workers' militia managed to dispose of the handful of intellectual rebels and counterrevolutionaries, before they got around to smashing up the editorial offices of the weekly papers, before a government of true and faithful Marxists could take over, committed to liquidating the revisionist gang on its own.

That first morning, contrary to what I had feared during the night, there was nothing to suggest that their expectations would be fulfilled. They had not yet announced the "true, proper government" on whose invitation they had come to help in bringing to naught the imperialist plots hatched by the counterrevolutionaries in collusion with imperialist espionage centers and West German revanchist elements. The Moscow radio had justified the invasion of Czechoslovakia by the five Socialist armies in high-sounding phrases about fraternal internationalism coming to the help of their class brothers; they had even mentioned "loyal Communists who had asked the allied armies to come to their aid," but without being able to name a single one of them. That morning I still did not believe they could be so muddle-headed; I thought they would be well informed about the real feeling among the people, the actual state of public opinion, and the true balance of forces in the Party itself, in the government, and among the people. I assumed that the vagueness of their statements was due to fears that angry crowds might do some harm to their "loyal" supporters. Nobody could have guessed, that first morning, that they had not succeeded in setting up any government, any leadership within the Party, and that they had not found one, not a single one, among the older conservative politicians who was willing to collaborate with them.

It is my opinion that the main credit for this should be given to the radio. From early that morning they were broadcasting appeals for unity, for loyalty to the Dubček leadership, calls for order, to beware of provocation; all who betrayed the people at such a grave time, all who lent themselves to collaboration with the occupation forces, should be pilloried.

"Citizens, do not buy up unnecessary supplies, you can upset economic life. Citizens, go to work normally; we must not allow the occupation to cause even greater damage to the country's life. Citizens, do not let yourselves be drawn by provocation. Keep calm! Do not give the occupation forces any excuse for armed action. Citizens, take care of your lives, every drop of blood spilled would be a great pity, everyone who was no longer with us would be missed. Show the invaders your scorn in silence, do not attempt to discuss or argue with them; they are at a loss, they do not know where they are or what they ought to be doing; they are nervous, and that is dangerous. The occupation forces are hungry and tired. Do not give them a crust of bread or a drop of water. Protect our common Socialist property from looting. Protect your own private property. Do not travel by car unnecessarily; the roads are crammed with military vehicles on the move; they are ruthless, and there already have been many accidents."

"Not a drop of water for the invaders" became the chief slogan of resistance, repeated over and over again by the free, legal transmitters that grew up like mushrooms all over the country after the regular studios had been seized and put out of action. That morning they were still broadcasting from their regular studios, and they succeeded in achieving the impossible: they kept the people calm, united as never before in their history, and bolstered up their morale, which had seemed so low during the night.

I felt I ought to be doing something, something positive; everybody ought to have something positive to do that day and the next. It was not likely that the radio could carry on in this independent fashion for long; we ought to be preparing for the worst, and there was not much time left.

I phoned the broadcasting studio.

"Would you like a statement?"

Of course they would, very much so; I should come as soon as I could, at once; they had been informed the building would soon be occupied and it might be within the hour.

There were not many people about in the streets, apart from the young demonstrators. Their eyes were angry, and also afraid, uncertain, and infinitely sad. And infinitely reproachful as they watched the steel monsters standing there ready to shoot up the town on order. That morning people were so kind to each other, almost gentle, as if each felt the need to help his neighbors; every kindness was repaid with sincere smiles of gratitude. This nation was not on its knees, not by a long way!

You could hardly get past the Slovak National Council building, near the broadcasting studios, for the tanks standing there.
There were people around each of them, trying to convince the
Russian soldiers that they should go away, explaining that nobody had invited them to come and that their leaders had misled
them—in our country there was no counterrevolution to be suppressed. Very few of the young men in the tank crews dared to
answer, but the little that was said revealed a great deal. Most of
them did not even know where they were or what they were
supposed to be doing. Some of them thought they were on
maneuvers, others were under the impression they were in
Hungary. Two or three days later, in Central Bohemia, they
were going to be surprised at how well the people spoke Czech,
because they thought they were in West Germany in order to
kill off the hydra of Fascism. I pushed my way through the
throng. The program editor I had spoken to on the phone was
waiting anxiously in the doorway, and he took me straight to the
recording studio to tape my statement; they would be sending it
out in a little while. In the corridor we met the actor who had
just finished reciting fighting, rebellious poems of the last century, in the tradition of Janošík, the outlaw hero. A voice came
from the loudspeaker, a writer friend doing his bit; he, too, and
not only he, but all the writers, would be thinking the same and
doing the same. We had been squabbling among ourselves not
so long ago, but that was forgotten now. . . .

I wanted to be brief—why waste words? I urged my listeners
to stick together and maintain order.

"Behave as though you haven't seen them, haven't heard
them—as though they were not here. . . ."

I did not manage to finish. Someone came in and said calmly:
"They're here." We had all known they would not be long in
coming, but only the technician panicked and erased my statement from the tape. Never mind. At the same moment different people have the same thoughts. The next morning the
legal Prague transmitter would be broadcasting words that were
to become one of the main slogans of resistance:

"Show your scorn for the occupation armies by ignoring
them. Let the slogan of the day be: See nothing, hear nothing,

know nothing . . . answer all questions by *'Neponimayu. . . .'* "

I was downhearted as I left the building. They had silenced the voice of freedom in Bratislava and they would silence it everywhere. Even so, our thanks should go to the brave announcers and news editors; they had held up magnificently. If we meet again, Ondrej Sarvaš, you know we did not get on together, and I never disguised what I thought of you—but if we ever meet again, I'd like to shake your hand. You found yourself in those days. You were a real man. They come forward in the hour of need. . . . For years I had felt you ought not to be in radio, ought not to be the chief there; but I was wrong. The last few hours had shown you were the best man who could have done the job.

There was an armored car guarding the entrance to the building now, with machine gunners at the ready. In the hall young Soviet soldiers were already standing with the safeties off their machine-pistols. Everyone was free to leave, without being checked out, but nobody was allowed in. There was a crowd gathering in front of the building, and I joined it. I saw a member of the Executive Committee of the Party. The Central Committee would be sitting within an hour, and so would the Slovak National Council. Nothing was lost, as yet; nothing would be lost if we managed to maintain this amazing unity. . . .

Would we be able to? Without the radio? If we could not move about, consult each other, take common action, a common stand? Wasn't it clear enough that it would not take the occupation forces long to sow confusion in the Party and the nation? Prague would give out incorrect information about the situation in Bratislava, and vice versa. It was clear they were determined to use all means possible, and they would not stop at a lie or two. . . . Who would be in a position to tell the people the truth?

On my way back to the friends' house where we had been given a bed, I wandered around the tanks, listening to what people were saying. The debating fever began to get hold of me, too, but I thought there was no point in arguing with these soldiers who were completely uninformed; in fact I had the feeling that they were deliberately left in ignorance about the reason for their invasion of Czechoslovakia. They sat there on their tanks and armored cars, afraid to look people in the face, patiently suffering the names they were being called and allowing the youngsters to paint antioccupation slogans and insulting words on their tanks; they sat behind their machine guns and gazed into the middle distance, each of them looking in a different direction. Were they ashamed? Or afraid?

I went from one tank to another.

Smotri v glaza . . . nu, smotri . . . —Look me in the eye . . . Come on look . . .

No. They did not dare. I spoke to more than a hundred of them, challenging them to look me in the eye, and only one found the courage to do so. He smiled *"Pochemu nyet"*—"Why not?"—but turned his gaze away again almost at once. They knew where they were and what they were there for, then. They had never seen such a strange and powerful unarmed resistance before. Many of those who attacked them with words and arguments could speak Russian well enough.

I suddenly felt the need to be mean and cruel. If they were, why shouldn't we be?

"You're here and your cities are being occupied by the Chinese," I insinuated to these tired men. And then I got an even more insidious idea.

"You're done for, you're marked men, you've been infected by the poison of counterrevolution. You've seen our cities, you've heard what we think, and that won't suit them back home. They'll send you all to Siberia, you'll all have to be brainwashed, like your fathers when they got back after winning the war in Europe."

I was not prepared for what happened next. One of the hippies surrounding the tank I had been trying to arouse in this way spoke up; he was young, his hair was long, he was dirty and flashily dressed.

"Leave them alone. Can't you see the state the poor buggers are in? They don't know a thing, not a thing. They got their orders and here they are. Don't fight against them—fight the men who sent them here."

The answer to this argument came in a volley of shots from

the next block, a long burst of machine-gun fire. Nobody ran for shelter, nobody stirred; it was quite a bit farther on. The hippy shrugged his shoulders. "They're just poor buggers, they don't know a thing, but they're armed to the teeth. Isn't it all the worse for that?"

"They're poor buggers" could be heard often enough in the streets of Bratislava in the next few days, especially after it got around that they hadn't been given anything to eat. Even from the military point of view, the operation was not entirely brilliant, as I had supposed it was the night before. . . . Or did the Russian marshals really think the people were going to take their troops home and entertain them with sincere and affectionate hospitality?

An absurd thought came into my head: suppose they made a mess of the whole thing, suppose they didn't manage to get anybody on their side. They were making a mess of things from the start—suppose they had no alternative government prepared, suppose they'd based their plans on false reports, false information from Soviet espionage and diplomatic sources? Suppose a miracle were to happen and this amazing unity of the people behind Dubček and Svoboda, for freedom, could be kept up for a few days more? Would they think better of it? Would they retreat? They could not retreat, that was clear; they had come and they would stay a long time, and in the end they would get their way. But at what price? Would it pay them, this barbarous, cynical, useless and most unwise action? Would they not soon be cursing the day they began it all?

All through the previous year, when I was miles away from home and then when I got back to my own country, people had asked me the pessimistic question: suppose the Russians invade Czechoslovakia?

"That's out of the question, they wouldn't do it. That would mean the end of international Communism. It's impossible, out of the question, absurd." It is true that politics often are absurd, illogical, impossible and stupid—almost more often than not. With that reservation I rejected the idea.

But they did dare, they did come, and here they were.

They came, and the fantastic reason they gave for it would have done credit to Yelochka Shchukinová in Ilf and Petrov's famous satire. Yelochka Shchukinová, you may remember, got through the whole of her life with a vocabulary of eighty words, including the words *ech, och, ach* and *ich*. Compared to the vocabulary of Soviet propagandists, hers was amazingly rich. On every possible and impossible occasion, they churn out the same few terms: imperialist conspiracy, revisionism, counter-revolution, revanchism, imperialist aggression. In their arrogant vanity with its oversimplified categories, they imagine these words are enough to convince the world.

They are not alone in this. The Chinese Communists are now trying to convince the world that "Soviet revisionists and imperialist renegades" are plotting with the American imperialists to crush world revolution. To this end they are willing to join with anybody, even with the renegade Tito. What has the Soviet press been printing these days? The Chinese Communists are plotting with the American imperialists and the Tito revisionists to discredit in the eyes of the world the "fraternal international aid" given by the armies of the five Warsaw states to Czechoslovakia.

The circle has closed. In the eyes of the Chinese the Soviet Communists are revisionist traitors, allies of the imperialists; the Yugoslav Communists are revisionist traitors and allies of the imperialists; the Czechoslovak revisionists are counterrevolutionary traitors and allies of the revanchists and imperialists. In the eyes of Moscow this is quite correct, except for one small detail: it is the Chinese who are the allies of the revisionists, imperialists, and so on. . . . Yelochka Shchukinová would say, "Ech!"

The insensitive attitude of Soviet politics, its inability to appreciate what tact and good taste require, allowed and made possible something more than usually monstrous. Czechoslovakia was invaded not only by Soviet tanks, but also by tanks from Poland, Hungary, and East Germany, when most of the Czechs and Slovaks still remember the invasion of their country by these armies in 1938, after Munich. The only difference is that then they came as an invading enemy, while today they claim to be "class brothers." Tanks in the role of class brothers is something new in world politics. In all cases to date when the frontiers of an independent state were invaded, it was an enemy state that was attacked. From now on things will be different; the diplomatic vocabulary is out of date and needs expanding; the word "occupation" should be replaced by "help given to class brothers." It sounds more dignified. If the proposal were to come before the UN Security Council, none of the Great Powers would be likely to veto it. Let the words "aggressor," "occupation" be reserved for little states like North Vietnam or Israel. The best would probably be to call Czechoslovakia the aggressor against the five Socialist countries. What is so absurd about that? Perhaps we shall live to see it before long. . . . Our "class brothers" discovered American arms dumps in this country. They may discover all sorts of things yet. Maybe they will get hold of Czechoslovak military plans revealing that Eduard Goldstücker, Jan Procházka, Antonín Liehm, Pavel Kohout, Milan Kundera, Arnošt Lustig, Ladislav Mňačko, outwardly writers but in reality the generals of a secret invasion army, planned to occupy Budapest, Warsaw, Sofia, East Berlin —and Moscow. I am willing to confess to this side of my counterrevolutionary activities in advance, quite openly. I had planned to make my Moscow headquarters in the Ukraine Hotel, that magnificent piece of architecture, from whence I intended to direct my Zionist conspiracy for world domination. Once again—for the third time in my short life—I am a Jew. . . .

Is it so impossible? Nothing is impossible. A few weeks ago I thought it was impossible that the friends and allies of Czechoslovakia would invade and occupy her. In politics everything is possible. . . .

There are even proofs, after all! On the streets of all the bigger Czechoslovakia towns you can see signposts prepared for the needs of this secret invasion army: in Bratislava you can read "Moscow 1,950 km.," "Budapest 160 km.," and follow signposts showing the roads to Warsaw, Sofia and Berlin. Not that the Czechoslovak counterrevolutionaries were going to be content with that; their plans were far-reaching indeed: the Crimea! Siberia! even the Solovetski Islands! That would be right up their street, to turn this little White Sea paradise into a polar concentration camp for all loyal revolutionaries and class brothers!

Does it sound so absurd? The population of Czechoslovakia bears roughly the same ratio to that of the Soviet Union as does the population of Israel to that of the Arab countries. Yet was it not the plan of the Zionists, encouraged by their international imperialist paymasters and particularly by the West German revanchists, to march on Damascus, Cairo, and Amman in order to achieve their aggressive ends, which were frustrated only by the consistent anti-imperialist policy of Moscow? *Pravda* itself said so, in Moscow. And when the gang of Zionists was unsuccessful in one direction, they decided to make a general attack on the freedom of the nations and on world peace, against progress, by occupying Moscow and other Socialist capitals. Now they were trembling in powerless anger and in fear, for the vigilant fist of our class brothers had discomfited them, with its fraternal aid to the Czechoslovak people! The world did not yet know all, but it soon would. The whole truth! It would be revealed in all its nakedness by *Literaturnaya Gazeta,* by *Pravda,* and *Izvestia.* The illegal radio transmitters of the Czechoslovak counterrevolutionaries were inciting world opinion against the Soviet Union, trying to turn the truth upside down with their lying propaganda. Broadcasting from revanchist West German stations, too! Fortunately there is still the Vltava transmitter, the only legal one, broadcasting the truth to the people of Czechoslovakia in a Czech and a Slovak such as they have never heard before. The people can learn from this source that they have been greeting their armored friends and brothers with grateful enthusiasm, that they are rejoicing to see the mortal danger of counterrevolution driven from their door. Tass photographers have even caught these historic moments for posterity: a Soviet soldier, Ivan, our dear well-beloved Vanushka, with a smiling child in his arms; a group of students in cheerful conversation with the sons of their liberators in the streets of

Bratislava; towns decorated with flags to welcome the liberators (it is not difficult to touch up the flags flying at half-mast, Soviet photographers have tidied up worse things than that in their time); people are weeping with relief and emotion on the sidewalks . . . nor will they miss the historic moment when a muscular tank gunner tries to teach his Slovak friend how to roll a cigarette in a piece of newspaper. . . . True, if Soviet propagandists bother with this sick invention of my perverted Zionist brain, they can easily prove I am lying. Soviet soldiers no longer roll these cigarettes, which may be taken as proof of the "truthfulness" of my statement (the quotes were added by *Pravda*).

A magnificent shot, a wonderful piece of evidence! A crowd of patriotic youngsters in the streets of Bratislava, with the flag at their head; they are singing the "International," and at the sound and sight of them the counterrevolutionary rats have gone back into their holes (a quarter of an hour later an armored car poured machine-gun bullets into this crowd of patriotic youngsters as they enthusiastically welcomed their class brothers. A seventeen-year-old girl student was killed).

The heroic Soviet war photographers, alas, caught less joyful sights, proving how low the Slovak counterrevolutionaries have sunk. Under cover of darkness the Slovaks have painted across walls in the city their emblem of battle, a red star with the Nazi swastika in it. You see how far their alliance with the West German revanchists has gone! They are painting swastikas over the walls! Struck with fear by the resolute action of our brothers, however, the cowards are masking their true aims under apparently peaceful slogans. NEUTRALITY! What does this word mean in Czechoslovak conditions? Neutrality means breaking away from the Warsaw Pact, annulling treaties of alliance, handing Czechoslovakia over to the mercies of the revanchists. That cannot, must not be allowed! That was why they had come, to prevent such a thing from happening. The holy cause of defense of internationalism is near to the heart of all true Communists, all revolutionaries. They would not be fulfilling their historic destiny if they looked on powerless while the freedom of Czechoslovakia, so dearly bought, was strangled in the clutches of the counterrevolution!

These are not the only words chalked up on walls. "Wake up, Lenin, Brezhnev's gone mad!" "Our friendship has been deepening so long, we've finally struck rock bottom." The Russian reporter cannot read these words, though, cannot understand them. They are a vast nation with no need to imitate others; their own language and their own alphabet are enough for them. What about the words written in Azbuka, though? At every step, on every square, every street, every house, every shop window, it is there written in Russian characters: *Rusye domoy*. That is only wishing them a good journey home after their exemplary military exercise. And the many quotations from Marx and Lenin to be seen written up, especially the one from Marx that says no nation can be free that crushes the freedom of others— they only show how well educated in Marxism the Czech and Slovak people are, particularly the most loyal of them, and that they will never allow Czechoslovak counterrevolutionaries to crush the freedom of the Russian people!

Look, the Czechoslovak working class has not been misled by crimes of the counterrevolutionaries! The street sweepers go about their work every day, and even seem more enthusiastic than they used to be; Stefanik Street, which was under repair, where the counterrevolutionaries had damaged the streetcar rails, is being finished off with concrete as though nothing had happened; the people waiting in the line for bread to be delivered are pretty quiet; the city transport repairmen are at work on the trolleys. Is not all this proof that the hard-working Czechoslovak people have only one thought in the world? To live in peace? The factory workers are trying to make up for the damage done to production by the counterrevolution; work goes on, transport is getting moving, too. Only those loudly dressed, long-haired hooligans will keep on trying to provoke the peaceful Soviet soldiers. . . .

Soviet reporters and photographers will have all this in their records for posterity; whether it will appear in the Soviet press remains to be seen. It may yet be necessary to explain away the fraternal aid as a dress rehearsal by the Warsaw Pact command for defense of Czechoslovakia against the threat of invasion. . . .

For no government has been set up. There is no government in the country at all. The announcers of the Czechoslovak radio, whom the Russians have failed to silence though they have occupied their buildings and taken over their equipment, are repeating this fact hour by hour.

"It is half-past eleven, exactly twelve hours since the occupation armies entered Czechoslovakia. The Soviet occupation forces have still not been able to give the names of anyone who 'called on them for help,' or to set up a new, collaborationist government."

That evening Hannah and I went around to sleep with friends. We could easily have gone home; there was no reason to suppose they would start arresting yet. We should not have slept, though, in spite of this practical certainty; every creak, every rustle, every tiny sound would have startled us. I went out to look around the streets again in the evening. Some were quite empty, while in others students were hard at work sticking up more posters, portraits of Dubček and Svoboda, and scrawling more slogans. There was not a house, not a shop window that was not covered. The cafés, bars, and restaurants closed at nine. Armed Soviet patrols were out in the streets, and guards armed with machine guns were on duty in front of government buildings. The black silhouette of Soviet machine gunners could be seen against the starry sky on some roofs. Here and there shots were heard. In the lounge of the Devin Hotel, the foreigners were sitting around in silence. I tried to order a brandy, but the girl at the bar said: "We are not serving alcoholic drinks."

Nobody had given any order. Nobody was giving any orders at all. People knew of their own accord what ought to be done. Each and every one of them was his own government, with its orders and regulations, while the government itself was somewhere very far away, probably in Moscow. Everything the occupation forces tried to paralyze went on working and even worked better than in normal times; by the evening the people had even managed to deal with the bread situation. They obeyed the radio call not to lay in excessive supplies.

There were very few cars in the streets that night, and only here and there groups of people stood talking. But when I got to a side street running alongside a park, where there were no tanks, I stopped in surprise. Lovers were necking on the seats; an old man with a stick came out for his usual evening walk; it was idyllic, peaceful . . . even the occasional shot seemed very far away.

I went to bed early. Hannah sleeps lightly and restlessly, but the excitement of the last twenty hours must have been too much for her. She was fast asleep, breathing regularly, and did not stir. I did not feel sleepy. I lay looking up at the ceiling and the flickering shadow of branches across the bars of the half-closed Venetian blinds.

I wanted to be absolutely clear in my mind about everything. When do you need to be clear about things, if not at a time like this?

The occupation took me by surprise, and yet I had been prepared for it. Politics are not realistic, everything can happen, had been my answer when people asked what the Russians were going to do. I had not believed they would do it, but I could not exclude the possibility. And they had done it.

I wanted to go over the whole of our plight from all angles. I did not expect to discover any unknown truths about it; I had spent much time and thought on all that had happened here during my lifetime, but now, when there was nothing to do but wait and see what was going to happen next, it was a good moment to draw up and balance the account. There was nothing else I could do. A writer who cannot speak to his public and cannot publish is powerless. I had signed the declaration by the Slovak writers that afternoon, like many other writers, and it was certainly not the last statement I would be signing. But even if the periodicals I published in were to appear, they could not print my work. After my adventure in Israel I was the classic example of a counterrevolutionary, and every public statement I made would prove to the occupation forces that I was plotting underground. I was condemned to silence. To keep silent, though, does not mean to stop thinking . . . almost the reverse.

The exiles returned. They were brought in 1945 from Moscow to Košice, not long after the Red Army had liberated this eastern Slovak metropolis, since 1938 assigned to Hungary. The military command released for their use a small mansion in the park near the railway station. From here they began to rule over their still oppressed country. There they agreed on the program that, as they thought, would best meet the needs of the country and the wishes of the people.

The nation welcomed them frenetically. Why not? The exiles Tomáš Masaryk and Beneš, both in exile, had persuaded the states of the entente, France, Great Britain and the United States, to establish and recognize the Czechoslovak Republic. Now Masaryk was long dead, but Beneš, Eduard Beneš, the President of the Czechoslovak Republic at home and except for a short interval the President of the Czechoslovak Republic in exile, had returned for the second time in his life as the liberator of his country. There can be no doubt that this clever diplomat achieved the most favorable conditions the victorious Allies could be persuaded to give Czechoslovakia. It was not an easy task. Part of the country, the eastern part, had become an obedient vassal state after the breakup of the Republic; this vassal state of Hitler's was at war with the Allies. *De jure* this state existed; up to the outbreak of war the Western powers had maintained diplomatic missions in Bratislava; but Beneš had managed to achieve subsequent annulment of the state, as though it had never existed. This view was accepted even by the Soviet Union, which had maintained an embassy in Bratislava up to the time of the invasion of the Soviet Union by Hitler.

Beneš had achieved even more than this. He obtained from the signatories of the Munich agreement the annulment of this agreement. Those who had signed it themselves declared it invalid. Czechoslovakia, the first state to be attacked and broken up by Hitler after Austria, won for herself the status of a victor. It is not important what her representatives felt about it.

Who could have asked for more? Beneš, the President-Liberator, was greeted by the whole Czech and Slovak nations with delighted ovations.

That he returned to govern a people who meanwhile had become strange to him, neither he nor the people could guess.

The exiles returned. For six years they had been cut off from the people for whose freedom they had been fighting and taking diplomatic action, to the best of their ability, and whose future they had tried to settle around conference tables in London and in Moscow, without any very precise knowledge of what this people thought about things and what they wanted for themselves.

There, outside the country, they had decided on how the country should be run after the war. There, outside the country, they had distributed all the important ministerial portfolios. There, outside the country, they had agreed (not without unpleasant squabbling) that the four political parties "allowed" to exist in exile, because each of them belonged to one, should be equally represented in the government and in the National Assembly.

Beneš and his loyal supporters could rejoice in their victory; it was a real victory, a clever political move in view of the fact that it might be the Red Army (and according to a clause in the Yalta Agreement, which was not yet public, *was* to be the Red Army) that would liberate Czechoslovakia from Nazi domination. What the people at home thought about this "parity," they did not know and did not seem to care. They bargained with the Moscow Communist group and gained the maximum they could in conditions that were not favorable to them. Throughout the war Beneš balanced skillfully between London and Moscow, between Churchill and Stalin. He had his reward. Czechoslovakia would not be "altogether" Red. As for the rest, time would tell. That was the most that could be gained for the moment.

Yet Czechoslovakia, as far as the vast majority of her people was concerned, and that included the farsighted members of the bourgeoisie, was already prepared and ripe to turn Red. The exhausted nation, robbed of the most elementary rights, betrayed by its Western allies, swayed by sentiment and spontaneous sympathy, was longing for the arrival of the Red heroes, Stalin's eagles, who would bring with them not only freedom, but also Socialism as well—a Socialism for which this nation had already shown strong inclinations. In spite of an extraordinary degree of persecution, the Communist Party had never ceased to be the one organized resistance force throughout the cruel years of the occupation of the country. The point is not what the Communists had achieved, although they had achieved plenty, by organizing, declaring, and carrying out the Slovak National Rising. In the minds of the people the Communists were the main power and the chief hope of all resistance, if only because the Nazis were so incredibly and methodically determined to wipe them out. After the liberation the Communist Party of Czechoslovakia presented its accounts to the nation: twenty-eight thousand executed, tortured, beaten to death—mostly active Party members, two-thirds of the prewar membership of the Party. Whenever anything went wrong for the Nazis in Bohemia, Moravia, or Slovakia, people whispered, "It was the Communists . . ." and in most cases they were right. By the work and behavior of its members during the occupation, the Communist Party had won the respect and admiration of the people. This naturally created an atmosphere favorable to Socialist ideas as the ideal social and political system for the country once it would be free again. There were many capitalists who fell in with this enthusiastic view, some sincerely, others because they realized that in fact they would have no alternative, since it was the Russians who would be liberating the country.

In May, 1945, the political situation in Czechoslovakia was ripe for the declaration of a Socialist constitution. People were still suffering from the mood of days spent in cellars, anxiously praying that God might take their all, so long as He left them their lives. Gottwald could have organized a plebiscite: straightforward Socialism, yes or no? The vast majority would have said yes. Gottwald did not do it. A few months later such a plebiscite would have been a risky undertaking. The reactionaries had got over their initial shock, the Red Army had left Czechoslovak territory, Beneš had "slowed down" the realization of the minimum Socialist program—the nationalization of key industries—wherever and whenever he could.

In May, 1945, the whole Czech people welcomed with open arms the dirty, dusty Red Army men, welcomed them with real affection (the Red Army had come to Slovakia earlier and under different circumstances). The liberators did not need to rape women, the women fell on their necks of their own accord. I saw a well-built eighteen-year-old girl pull a Red Army man out of line and take him off to her room, almost by force. When he emerged, red-faced and breathless, he swore that the bitch told him to send more of them in. . . . This was indeed the only city in Europe where Red Army officers found the doors of the best homes open to them; each had its Russian, for entertainment, to prove his political reliability, for protection. Exhausted, filthy with dust and sweat, marching through the towns they had liberated, often they could not move forward through the rejoicing citizens thronging the roads and showering them with flowers, kisses, love, gratitude; oh, you angels, we've waited so long for you, here you are at last, we knew you'd come, we knew it'd be you, it could only be you, you grand lads, our Slav brothers, our liberators, Stalin's eagles! Many a unit literally disappeared, led off by the people to their homes. You're tired, come and have a rest, we haven't got much but what we have is all yours—a bottle of plum brandy saved for the occasion, it's yours; a bed, lie down and rest, don't bother to take off your boots; we'll turn a blind eye if your hands creep up beneath our women's skirts, you can have our daughters . . . why ask so roughly for our wristwatches, you can have them, take them for a souvenir. . . .

Over my head the radio called, softly but clearly: "Not a drop of water! Don't give them a drop of water!"

In splendid isolation in Moscow, Gottwald the exile had thought up a strategic plan to bring his Party the final victory.

A far greater victory than he dreamed of was there for the taking, but he failed to recognize it.

More than once in the years that followed, I wondered why.

Did he not trust the will of his own people? Did he expect the idea of Socialism to meet with far more resistance? Did he think it would have to be fought for first? Why in the first speeches he made did he repeat over and over again that the Party's aim was to gain the majority of the nation in support of their program, when that majority was already in favor, without any doubt?

Did this fact fail to fit in with the ambitions of the Great Strategist and Revolutionary Leader? Did a revolution that came so easily and spontaneously, without his active and visible contribution, seem too insignificant? Did he love a fight and want the chance to shine? Was he a romantic, dreaming of barricades and himself in a hail of bullets?

Or was he a dogmatist carrying out his revolutionary theory regardless of the real facts, decreeing a fight for national liberation led by the Communists and passing into a Socialist revolution by degrees? That was the way they stuffed it down our throats at courses on politics; even the October Revolution was preceded by the bourgeois democratic revolution of February.

It is difficult to guess today what he thought then. All I know is that when in 1947, in the Party School, I criticized the tactics of the Party and said that we had lost a favorable opportunity to set up the dictatorship of the proletariat in the weeks after the liberation, I was threatened with disciplinary action for such heresy. The nation was not ripe for such a fundamental change, I was told; the people had to be won over.

That was what I was told in the presence of my fellow students, but later that evening, inviting me to go for a stroll with him, the head of the school cautiously let me see that he really agreed with what I had said.

At the risk of being blamed for the unhistorical words, "if only," I make so bold as to say: the nation was ripe, the nation wanted Socialism then. There are millions of living witnesses, so long as they are willing and able to remember exactly what they thought then. In Czechoslovakia, and this needs no "if only," Socialism would have followed another path, not the thorny one it was soon called upon to take

It may not have been Gottwald's mistake. Something may have been due to Stalin's respect for Beneš. Perhaps the man of steel felt like being generous and patient with Czechoslovakia, or perhaps he was afraid of upsetting the regimes in Poland, Hungary, Bulgaria, and Romania—Stanislaw Mikolajczyk, Ferencz Nagy, King Michael. Perhaps it was Stalin who did not know exactly what to do and how to do it in Eastern Europe. There was no Cold War yet, in 1945, and the Great Powers at least tried to look as though they intended to carry out their solemn obligations. And among those obligations, as we know now, was one giving the Western powers a partial influence in this region by setting up and preserving compromise governments there.

Whatever the reason, once again the Czechoslovak people could not decide their fate entirely for themselves.

Not quite three years later the Socialist revolution in Czechoslovakia, on the surface inspired and called forth by a government crisis, was a fairly hazardous undertaking. The legality of Gottwald's government was in the balance, and a demonstration of strength was necessary.

The whole of the non-Communist Western world called February, 1948, a Communist putsch, and still calls it so. They were wrong. February, 1948, wrought fundamental and decisive political changes in Czechoslovakia, but absolutely legally. Nobody can blame the Communists for turning to their own advantage a unique situation which they had not brought about, and against which they had issued repeated warnings. Nor can the Communists be blamed because the Czechoslovak state was headed at the time by a President who let his supporters down at the decisive moment, for the second time. He was not the Communists' President; he was the exponent and chief hope of the anti-Communist policy of the Western powers. Beneš, the undecided "master of compromise," did not use the powers he had under the Constitution. When the ministers representing the bourgeois parties resigned, he could have asked Gottwald to hand in the resignations of the whole of his government. There is no reason to suppose that the Communists would have given way in this struggle for power, or that they would have been defeated, but in such a case the world would have been right to use the word "putsch."

It was Beneš who preserved the appearance of legality for the Communist revolution. Not only did he respect Gottwald's incomplete government with the portfolios of the departed ministers unassigned, but he signed the list of members of the new government of the reorganized National Front, as Gottwald put it before him. This may not be to the liking of the fanatical anti-Communists, but it is none the less the fact of the matter.

The Communists did not even have to try very hard. A few mass demonstrations in Wenceslas Square, with the thermometer twenty-seven degrees below zero, were sufficient proof of what the people wanted; three hundred thousand people came to the great demonstration in the Old Town Square. All they had to do was to stick up the slogan that anyone who left the National Front government was putting himself outside the great coalition of his own accord, and signing away his right to decide the fate of the people. The Communists had pointed out their attitude several weeks earlier, when there was only a hint of crisis in the government. They could quote on their side the agreement signed among all four political parties, to the effect that all misunderstandings and differences of opinion would be settled by discussion in the "supraparty" organization of the National Front which included mass organizations such as the youth and trade-union organizations, as well as political parties.

However absurd it may sound, the Communists at that time wanted to deal with such differences by means of discussion and compromise. It could do them no harm. The real cause of the February crisis was the fact that the leaders of the bourgeois parties were afraid of the coming elections to the National Assembly. In the elections to the temporary National Assembly, held in 1946, the Communists had gained a majority such as they had never enjoyed in democratic elections before or were to afterward. In Bohemia and Moravia (political conditions in Slovakia were somewhat different) they won 43½ percent of the votes, enough to guarantee the premiership for Gottwald. Immediately after the elections Gottwald announced his new program, that of winning over the absolute majority of the country for the Party's program, that is to say the Socialist program. This would confirm the Party's majority, thus giving the first chance ever to a Communist Party to carry out a revolutionary program on the basis of a legal parliamentary majority. But the bourgeoisie, taking advantage of the bad economic situation in the country after the war years, did not give the bourgeois parties its confidence and financial support to be defeated by the Communists. And when Gottwald's aim of gaining the support of the absolute majority for his program seemed to be not only possible, but also very likely, the leaders of the clerical People's Party and of the pink National Socialist Party, once upon a time founded by Beneš himself, decided to leave the scene in their own way, and not be driven off by catastrophic election results. They would not otherwise have risked a government crisis only a few months before the new elections.

Maybe the idea that they were "forced out of office by a Communist putsch" was born in their own heads, and maybe it came from their Western advisers. In the atmosphere of the Cold War it would have been very unwelcome to the American and West European political leaders to see the Communists in power in a single country as the result of parliamentary elections. The leaders of the Czechoslovak bourgeois parties risked a split, although they could not have been so stupid as to ignore the Communist reaction to this exposed flank. There are plenty of documents from just before the crisis, in which the Communists warned them that if they left the National Front, the anger of the people would sweep them away.

It seemed to every thinking observer at the time that they were only too willing to let themselves be swept away, with the consent and aid of Beneš, or without it.

The reactionary bourgeois parties did not perish in a cruel, unequal fight against superior Communist strength, but melted away of their own accord; they simply ceased to exist as a real political power. Deserted by their bankrupt leaders, the party members began declaring support for the dynamic Communist program, whether out of calculation or out of enthusiasm. In fact this phenomenon had already appeared in no small measure before the crisis, and should have been a warning to their leaders not to leave the government under any circumstances. The Communists had constantly urged them to remain in the government; did this emphasis on the unity of the National Front appear to be maneuvering them into a desperate situation? However that may be, at this stage of the political struggle, the Communists acted far more cleverly than their opponents. Can they be blamed for that?

I was there. On that fateful day twenty years ago, I was in the Strakov Academy, the traditional seat of the government, from early morning until late at night. I wanted to see all the members of the government arrive and I wanted to see them leave. In the nervous chaos that reigned there, I witnessed many acts that, though quiet and dignified on the surface, were explosive in intent. They were still arrogant and proud in their public role of responsible statesmen. A day later a storm of popular anger swept them from office; two days later I was in the office of one of them, Hubert Ripka, when the workers' militia came to throw him out of it. Ripka in appearance and probably in honesty was above the rest of his colleagues; when the militia appeared in the doorway, he was sitting at his desk, tapping the table with a pencil. They need not have said anything; the formal order to leave the building at once and hand over the keys of his safe was unnecessary. He handed them over of his own accord. Getting to his feet, he put on his overcoat; maybe he felt like making an emotional farewell, but he shrugged it off. Still, he turned at the door and said: "Gentlemen, I wonder whether we're on our own in this or whether our allies are in the same boat." He was referring to Šrámek, the leader of the clerical People's Party; there did not seem to be much confidence in the ally.

He went away. Into exile for the second time. I always

thought he was wasted on the party he represented, but what other party could he have belonged to?

I saw the crash. With my own eyes I saw the chairman of the National Socialist Party booed out of the academy with such fury that he had to get away under police protection, showered with torn-up party cards. Such bankruptcy is rare in political life.

A more convincing proof of the legality of February than the formal diplomatic actions can be seen in the spontaneous expression of the will of the people. The unity of those weeks was far from being as absolute as it was after January, 1968, and the months that followed, but in many ways there is considerable similarity between the two periods. Then, too, twenty years back, the people took things into their own hands and accepted only those who were prepared to talk openly. For people who have never lived through such "days of truth," it is difficult to imagine the feelings you experience. More than once in the last few months I have heard many people say: "Well, these weeks were worth all the troubles we've been through."

Gottwald, then, was as popular a leader as Dubček twenty years later, though not so universally accepted.

I did not like him. He was undoubtedly a clever politician, rather slow and awkward, though a convincing speaker; he had a decided personality that won the respect of friends and enemies, but I did not like him. He was too obviously anxious to make a career, too unscrupulous in his delight at victory. There are things that can be said of a statesman, clever, characteristic remarks, but they should come from others. I did not like it when Gottwald, after nominating the new government in February, shouted:

"Gottwald is no Tuszar!" (Tuszar was the Social Democrat premier in 1919 and 1920, accused by the Communists of betraying the working class. It is a historical fact that he did not fulfill the hopes of the people that the young Republic would be a Socialist one.)

Nor did I like it when he declared to a demonstration of two hundred thousand on Wenceslas Square, on the day of his election as President.

"And now a worker President is sitting on the throne of the Kings of Bohemia!"

A stupid way to boast! The worker president of a Socialist country ought to rule from a modern building equipped with the most up-to-date telecommunications, both inside and out a fitting setting for all the new, modern, unique qualities that distinguish Socialism from what has gone before. The palace of the Kings of Bohemia is certainly one of the jewels of European civilization, and there is no reason why a worker president should not occupy it for a time, but there was no reason to rejoice over the fact.

I knew Gottwald intimately, and I knew the people round him. From the time he took over the leadership of the Party in 1929, he surrounded himself with young, efficient men, for the most part intellectuals; they formed a group of energetic Marxist thinkers. The Party worked successfully throughout the thirties, its strength and prestige increasing as the country felt more and more the threat of Hitler's Nazism. The people regarded the Communists as the most consistent fighters against Fascism, which indeed they were.

The Munich capitulation damaged neither Beneš nor Gottwald. They both returned as victors and for three years were the two leading personalities in the country. Although they were on opposite sides, it looked as though they were capable of working together. February, 1948, swept one of them off the stage; the Communists did not trust Beneš, and his own supporters reproached him with indecision and capitulation. Less than three months had elapsed when the National Assembly elected Gottwald to the position of President and Beneš retired into private life, to die soon afterward.

I was a young, ambitious reporter then, working for *Rudé Právo*. From the outset I had been successful. Later on, in Slovakia, I was to hear a doubtful compliment from a high official of the Party:

"When people read about our meetings and our public appearances, the reports in our newspapers somehow always seem dull and uninteresting, not a bit like the truth. You do it better; your reports always make it sound like a real event."

Perhaps. Perhaps it did sound like a real event, but it was not always so. It was my ability to "do it better" that lead me to find a spark of life in the dull three-hour speeches. Thus I "helped to produce" personalities who never were personalities. They soon discovered that I had this talent, and the door to many offices was open to me. Not only Communists sought me out; Laušmann, the Social Democrat leader, was another.

This was what brought me to Gottwald, or rather this talent of mine drew his attention to me.

He wanted me. When he wanted to be sure an idea would take on, when he wanted a boost for himself, he would ask the office to send me on the job. Sometimes he took me on long journeys in the presidential car, and I traveled hundreds of miles with him, just Gottwald, the driver and me. Sometimes I was told to come over to the government building, but it occasionally happened that he would stop by for me at the paper.

He always sat in front, by the driver. I would say good morning, and he would mumble a reply with the eternal pipe in his mouth. That was all. He never asked about my work, how things were on the paper, what the kids were doing . . . all he cared about was that I "did it better." This lack of personal interest was almost insulting; in his eyes I was a piece of furniture. Publicity is something necessary, and I do it a bit better; I was there to chronicle his greatness, his genius, his magnificent successes. Maybe he thought it was sufficient reward that it was I who was allowed and ordered to perform this duty. It takes quite a bit of arrogance to drive for hours and never say a word to your companion, as though he was not there. Especially for the hearty fellow Gottwald was supposed to be.

That was something that always jarred. When he wanted to, he could be hearty, jolly, embracing old Party members and calling them by their first names; they would be in seventh heaven because he hadn't forgotten them, that he even remembered their names. He would accept invitations to the homes of workers' families, praise the housewife's cooking, drink one or two glasses, and, when spirits rose, there'd be a song or two.

It was almost genuine, and only a man who knew him as well as I could have known that it was all put on, done for effect— for his public image. I could never be sure that this hearty, sincere image was not the genuine one, and the long silences in the car not simply the way he worked, meditating profoundly over the next steps to be taken, the next speech to be made. . . .

It was he himself who cured me of my doubts. I was in his office when the February crisis came to a head. He had seen me come in; when I greeted him he nodded, as much as to say, O.K., you can stay. I was there when Prokop Drtina handed in the resignation of all the ministers who were members of his party; I listened to Gottwald phoning orders to Rudolf Slánsky at Party headquarters; I was there when his private secretary came in to tell him there was a miners' delegation from the Most basin, come to express their support for him.

"They'll have to wait. Tell them to be patient; I've got some urgent business to attend to."

The "urgent business" was the telling of smutty stories. Events were proceeding of their own momentum, and there was nothing to be done but sit back and take note of them. Was he perhaps right? If he had received the miners' delegation at once, would it have made a bad impression? Might they not have thought he had nothing better to do than wait impatiently for them to appear?

He let them wait twenty minutes, then he got up and tidied himself inwardly and outwardly. I followed him out—it would make a good story, especially since Drtina had refused to receive the men only an hour before. I wanted to see it from the inside.

They welcomed him with roars of enthusiasm, and he had to raise his hands in protest to get them to be quiet.

"Welcome, comrades! Before we start business, I'd like to know who else is present besides the members of your delegation."

I was not a member of the delegation, nor was the reporter from the Bratislava paper *Pravda*. We both raised our hands.

Gottwald looked at us with suspicion. The miners near us looked at us with vigilant suspicion, too.

"Who are you, comrades?"

I muttered that I was from *Rudé Právo,* and the *Pravda* man gave his name, too. Gottwald relaxed with a smile.

"Well, comrades, I don't think we need have any secrets from our Communist papers. We can start talking."

I got up and left. I left in such a way that he was bound to see me go. When I turned in the doorway, he was glaring at me angrily. Nobody else noticed what had happened.

What a disgusting, cheap bit of comedy! Five minutes earlier we had been sitting opposite one another; he knew me well, by sight and by name.

Perhaps this "stage effect" occurred to him when he saw me among the miners; it would not have mattered, but he went too far. If he had just said: "So we've got *Rudé Právo* here with us," or something of that sort, it would have been enough. I was not more than five yards away from him, and he could not fail to recognize me. Why the melodrama? It did not fit in with his legend of statesmanship.

You may say it was a trifle, but I have learned to judge men by such trifles. A man may hold out for years, and then suddenly give himself away by just such a trifle. I did not kid myself that I was anything more to him than an impersonal chronicler, and he was never more to me than a Party member, a Party member who had been entrusted with the confidence of the Party for a time, as its Chairman. In the eyes of the Party and by Party rules we were equals; he was as bound to respect my existence as I was his.

I have never sought the favor of the great. The office a man holds does not impress me; I am more interested in who he is and what he has done to gain my respect. I was young and proud; I did not ask to be slapped on the back, but it insulted me to be denied, for whatever reason.

Later, in far more serious circumstances, Gottwald would deny others, would deny them one and all. After this trifling experience of my own I was not surprised.

I knew other "great" men, too, although I cannot explain how or why it came about. I never played any part in the Party apparatus, which was the criterion for these important people. I never played any part in social life, in the representative sense. All I was, to the very last, was an awkward, inquisitive journalist and writer with a sharply critical pen. Of all the "immortals," most of whose names have now fallen into oblivion, the one I knew best was Viliam Široký, the leading figure among Slovak Communists and for many years the Czechoslovak Prime Minister. He was friendly toward me, and I know that he twice saved me from imprisonment. This is surprising, for Široký cynically and mercilessly let his closest companions fall by the way without a word. I do not know of any other case in which he used his authority to stand by anyone in need. During the purge at the Ministry of Foreign Affairs, they criticized an elderly typist who many years before had served as secretary at the tiny illegal Party headquarters in Paris; she was accused of cosmopolitanism, and of being in touch with Vladimír Clementis (the Foreign Minister "purged" in 1950), who was then in Paris, before the outbreak of war. She called on Široký to testify in her favor, for he had been working in Paris at the time. Široký, Minister of Foreign Affairs, sat in judgment there, looking away and playing with a pencil; pretending to be elsewhere in his thoughts, occupied with other matters, he neither saw nor heard; he neither saw nor heard her when, dismissed in disgrace, she desperately called his name. A word would have sufficed to save her, but he did not speak.

It was from Široký's lips that I heard the terrible words that repelled me from politics and politicians for a long time:

"There is no friendship in politics."

He may have said it to justify his attitude toward the group of Slovak Communists who had just been removed from office and imprisoned. I cannot say. The time was to come when he would need friends, but his old friends had long since been destroyed by the pitiless purge machinery and there was no one, not a soul to stand by him or even to spare a word of pity for his sad fall. In the end his own defensive alibi was turned against himself.

I knew them all, more or less intimately, both the executed and their judges and executioners. There were all kinds among them, decent and dreadful. I had an almost inhuman hatred of Václav Kopecký, member of the Executive Committee, whom I considered the evil spirit in the Party, and his attitude to me was the same. Rudolph Slánsky, when he came in 1946 to quell a rebellion among the reporters on *Rudé Právo* against the imposition of an absolutely incompetent chief editor, shouted at me:

"You keep your mouth shut unless you want to land in prison!"

He did not even know my name; he knew nothing about me at all. My colleagues tried to persuade me to forget it; he'd only been excited. It is true that in the excitement of the moment you can do and say all sorts of things. But you can only threaten a man with prison if you are prepared to put him there and have the power to do so. It would be absurd for me to threaten anyone with prison, at any time. And Slánsky shouted his threat at me when the principle of parity was still in force, and when the laws were still there to be respected. No, there was no talking of Slánsky to me from that moment on. This little incident meant that, when they later accused him of all manner of crime, I was ready to believe them. A man who for nothing at all would threaten another with prison, although he knew not the first thing about him, was a man who would abuse his position and his power. A man who can abuse his power like that has no right to be in that position.

Čepička (while the Minister for Defense) tried to get me on his side. Prime Minister Antonín Zápotocký, although we rarely met and only in passing, liked me as I liked him. Karol Bacílek, who served a short time as Minister of Security, seemed to like my downright, impertinent criticism, although he was not spared it. Pavol David, feared all over Slovakia, feared me.

I was an awkward customer, brash, a journalist to be feared. There was no need to suppose the leading representatives of the

Party and the government were disinterested in their attitude toward me, nor did I conceal what I really thought of them, in my personal contacts with them, in public, or in what I wrote. They gnashed their teeth whenever my name was mentioned, and yet they incomprehensibly invited conflict. My very existence irritated them, and they put up with insults, contempt and ridicule from me. There were few, if any, who could dare what I got away with. Once, when President Antonín Novotný had been talking to the leading writers of the Writers' Union, he held me back for a few words. I do not know what led the "first in the land" to tell me what he would not have told anyone else.

He told me how Gottwald, Čepička, Slánsky, Široký, Bacílek, Rudolf Barák, then Minister of the Interior, and Kopecký had used all legal and illegal ways of getting as much personal power as they could.

"That's all very well," I interrupted him; "that's how things used to be. You put it across to the public, inside and outside the Party, as the struggle to uphold the unity and purity of the Party, its moral principles. And while you're talking about the way things were then, what about now, when those people have gone?"

He bridled like a turkey-cock and went away to the window. In a few moments he came back to me, boiling with suppressed fury, and started talking about something else.

"Do you remember when I held the post of Vice-Premier for a short while?"

I did. I nodded.

"Do you know why? The Central Committee was in session, and Gottwald suddenly turned to me in the middle of a discussion of something quite different. 'Tonda,' he said, 'you're going to be Vice-Premier, responsible for heavy industry. Make a good job of it, I warn you, or I'll have your neck, and you know I mean it.' "

"Sure," I told Novotný when he finished, "I always thought that was more or less the way things were up at the top."

That was indeed the way I imagined things. A group of people who had known each other for many years, who had lived together in the same hotel throughout the years in exile, who visited with each other's families and made dynastic marriages between their houses. People who knew each other's strong and weak points, who met almost daily at sessions of various bodies and institutions of government. They called each other by their first names, by nicknames, and exchanged intimate details of family life. They smiled at each other. They pretended profound affection for each other. And in reality they were only waiting, waiting for the moment when one could jump at the other's throat, break him, get rid of him.

Only a few months after Václav Kopecký had celebrated the fiftieth birthday of Rudolf Slánsky in an article, calling him "the finest son a Czech mother ever bore," this same Kopecký accused this same Slánsky of unheard-of crimes, calling him a Jewish Izzie and the spawn of darkest hell. Slánsky was arrested on his way home after having supper with Zápotocký. Supper was presumably a pleasant way of lulling the victim into a state of unsuspecting confidence. It would not do to have him return home unexpectedly, where they were just planting "incontrovertible evidence" of treason. His host, Zápotocký, must have known what was going on, all the time he was plying his guest. "Have another glass, Ruda, come on, just a little drop."

Yet Zápotocký, and I was not alone in thinking so, was by far the best and finest of the lot, and to this day, in spite of the blots on his escutcheon, his memory is respected and revered.

What had happened to these men of granite, these fighters who could take as good as they got? Everyone of them had a police record for political offenses, every one of them had been condemned to years of imprisonment by the judges of the prewar Republic. Everyone of them had been beaten up by the police, fought in street battles and demonstrations; the minute they got out of jail, they were back in the thick of it, inciting the workers against the authorities, organizing strikes, local rebellions, demonstrations, mass meetings. Karol Bacílek's police record even includes a warrant for his arrest on the charge of dynamiting the Strečno tunnels.

Those who did not succeed in emigrating in time, or who

were ordered by the Party to stay in the country and keep the underground work of the Party going, were the objects of special attention at the hands of the Gestapo. They held out, they survived it all, and maybe they would have survived even worse. The Brno Gestapo records say of prisoner Viliam Široký, "borrowed" for questioning:

"A fanatically obstinate Communist who organized political training inside a Slovak prison. Cannot be expected to break down."

Yet only a few years later these men were trembling before their Communist judges and pointing out to the prosecution that their crimes were even worse than they were accused of. The last time I went to see Široký, in 1958, I found this "fanatically obstinate Communist" who "cannot be expected to break down" sitting at his ministerial desk in a state of advanced schizophrenia, his gaze wandering and his expression seeming to ask: Who are you and what do you want? Spying? Or come to arrest me? What do you want from me, who has sent you after me, whom are you going to boast to about what you've got out of me?

I got up and said, "Comrade Prime Minister, I shall not be coming again."

Once so sensitive to insult, he seemed relieved.

What had happened to them? Where did their degeneration set in? When did they begin to fear and suspect everything and everybody? What had turned these fighting bulls into oxen humbly going to the slaughter?

Today I know the answer, more or less. It was power, the power they got their hands on, power neither their characters nor their training had prepared them for, power they did not know how to use. They were the romantic heroes of the proletariat, and today old comrades retired from active political life see them only in that light; they were capable of rebellion, they knew how to break down the system and the power that stood in their way; their long years of apprenticeship had taught them that. They were men of destruction, and their historic role was to destroy the evil old world. . . . In February, when they achieved their life's dream, the dream they had paid for with their youth and their private lives and happiness, when absolute power was at last put into their hands, they should have done the impossible, they should have done what is superhuman, or almost super-human: they should have said, we have done the needful, we have prepared a better life for you in the future. We should only be in the way now, and so we are handing over . . .

But who has ever left the stage at the height of his success? Had any of these men read Roman history and learned the lesson of the emperor who ordered his slave to draw his sword with his last words: the emperor must die erect? . . . And even if they had felt that way, who would have let it happen? The nation called in unison: Lead on, wise men, you are the only ones worthy of our confidence and affection.

And later on? Later on I had the privilege of seeing Karol Bacílek in a state nobody else knew of except his family. He was running about his apartment in black shorts, his whole body covered with an irritating red eczema.

"Why don't you retire?"

"Have you ever heard of retirement in our Party?" he snapped angrily.

He was right. There was no retirement in the Party. Those who left active political life either suffered from heart attacks, or—which was after all worse than a heart attack—from being dismissed, from shame and disgrace, and fantastic accusations.

I said nothing. There was no point in telling him, of all people, that, since there was no retirement in Party life, it was high time for him to put his house in order, so that retirement would be possible without fear that those left in office would jump at his throat, without fear of shadows. He would not have understood. He himself had been behind many such disappear-ances, even one where he himself, a few weeks earlier, had assured the comrade asking to be relieved of his job that the Party had full confidence in him.

February was the culmination of their stormy lives. Not long afterward one of them, despairing at the tasks ahead he knew to be beyond him, was to heave a sigh as he sat in his comfortable ministerial seat: "Oh, what good times those were!"

It was their task in February to change from one day to the next, to change everything around them and inside themselves. These destructive "tunnel saboteurs" of the past were now to be transformed into inspirers, creators and guardians of law and order; they would have to decide on the answers to thousands of urgent questions they had never thought about in their lives; they would have billions in their charge, at their disposal, billions the very thought of which dazzled them, used as they were to poverty; they would be expected to respect the law which they had always flouted; they would become the rulers, all at once they would be rulers. That was the furthest beyond their powers; neither their training nor their intellect was equal to that, nor were their characters, formed and determined by years of destructive activity.

Among them there were proletarians of the international type. My country? The worker has no country, he has only his chains. The only workers' country is the Soviet Union, where the working class has lost its chains. Only for this country, this workers' country, the only country worthy of men, were they willing to suffer, work, do all in their power. This fiction, this disease, had infected Communists all over the world. Where the interests of the Soviet Union clashed with the interests of their peoples, they were prepared to betray their own. This vast army of millions fanatically devoted to the cause were active and effective fighters. Neither Stalin nor those who succeeded him used this militant and morally unshakable force well. With the invasion of Czechoslovakia the last threads binding the Communist movement to Moscow in sentimental discipline are tearing now. This will not hurt the nations concerned; this emotional yet extreme discipline, which led even to self-destruction, was something unnatural and, at some points in history, an absurd and monstrous phenomenon. In the eyes of the Kremlin, these Communists were never equal partners. Moscow made use of them and misused and abused them; the carefully fostered internationalism of Communists all over the world served only to strengthen the international position of the Soviet Union, and more than once this was against the interests of other nations. The Communist parties and the organizations that sympathized with them were an enormous help to the Soviet Union in the most difficult years of her existence, nor was this help always in the interests of the world Communist movement or the Communist parties in the different countries. Communists were often called upon to support policies which they did not understand, which went contrary to their experience, to their desires and even to their moral principles, but strict Party discipline prevailed. Without explanation and without sufficient information, they were called upon to praise one day what they had been forced to condemn the day before. They were forced to swallow the incomprehensible pact with Hitler Germany. The main reason for the tragedy of Vladimír Clementis was his protest at that time against a pact that however explicable on the grounds of strategy was nevertheless immoral. The Communists were forced to accept and sanction the aggressive war against little Finland.

Czechoslovak Communists had even worse to come. When the invasion of Poland took place, their own country had already been invaded and occupied, the members of the Communist Party arrested and dragged off to concentration camps, pitilessly murdered and sadistically tortured by the Nazi machine of terror. When France and England declared war on Hitler, Stalin called it an imperialist war which was not in the interests of the working class. Bound by their strict discipline, the Communists had to act in accord with the German-Soviet pact. At the outbreak of war Czechoslovak units had been formed both in France and in England. The Czechoslovak government-in-exile in London had called up all able-bodied Czechoslovak citizens to serve in these newly formed units. After the Spanish Civil War was over, a large number of Czechoslovak Communists who had managed to escape from Madrid and cross the Pyrenees reached France. In addition there were many Communists who had emigrated to the West to escape the Nazis, or on Party orders; Communists could not emigrate to whatever country they wanted, but were assigned by a center in Cracow, some to

Moscow and some to London. Later on those who had been sent to London on Party orders paid for it heavily. All the "Western *émigrés,*" including the Communists, were suspect and subject to persecution. The Moscow leadership of the Czechoslovak Communist Party in exile issued a terrible order: Communists were not to take part in the imperialist war! Czechoslovak Communists were not to join the army; they were to disobey the government-in-exile. In France and England internment camps were set up for Czechoslovak Communists who refused to serve when called up. The fate of their country was to take second place, and so it did, if not in their hearts, at least to all appearances; this was the consequence of strict Party discipline.

Their attitude did not change until the day when the imperialist war changed overnight into a patriotic war. After the invasion of the Soviet Union by Hitler, the interned Communists asked to join the Czechoslovak Army in the west, or went to the USSR where the present President, General Ludvik Svoboda, then a colonel, was organizing an independent Czechoslovak unit. It must be said that the Communists in all these units fought splendidly, both in the east and in the west; it was in the interests of Moscow, and at last it harmonized with their own convictions and conscience.

That was the way Stalin saw proletarian internationalism; without a single doubt, without a single thought of their own, without the slightest resistance, Communists all over the world were to obey him, and they did.

The 1968 occupation of Czechoslovakia by the armies of the five Socialist states has torn the mask of internationalism from Soviet policy and diplomacy. The Soviet Union has taken its stand in the appropriate fashion side by side with the only other great power fit to be its partner, the United States. In vain did we warn against such a step, here in Czechoslovakia; in vain in many interviews did I say I did not fear Soviet invasion because it would mean the end of the international Communist movement. In vain did I write in one Czechoslovak weekly, that Czechoslovakia is not Santo Domingo, is not Guatemala. The

Soviet Party leaders and heads of government decided to go their own way, ignoring the warnings of Luigi Longo, Tito, Nicolae Ceausescu and other Communist leaders. The Soviet Union's aggression against Czechoslovakia was an act of which her enemies had long considered her capable, but which Communists did not want to believe possible, an act of imperialist aggression. An act that was even worse for being aimed at a small and friendly country, loyal to Socialism and to her allies, a country that had a pact of mutual aid with the Soviet Union signed in the belief that the Soviet Union would protect her sovereignty, freedom and independence with its strength and prestige. In return for this protection, of which we were never in doubt, this little country was to be the buffer and first battlefield if imperialist aggression against the Socialist world ever took place. It was a pact of mutual advantage. We relied on Soviet aid, but we, our territory, would be the first battlefield.

Whatever aspects of their plans did not work out, there was one thing the Kremlin must have known: that the occupation of Czechoslovakia would meet with the firm opposition of the European Communist parties, that the Soviet Union was surrendering its position at the center of the international working-class movement, that it was abandoning the line of proletarian internationalism.

In Moscow, the Russian leaders must have taken this possibility into account; this was in fact what happened. There can be no excuse that imperfect information from the diplomatic service gave the Kremlin a distorted view of the real situation; Longo, and other European Communist leaders, had warned the Kremlin openly and clearly. That the Soviet leaders took no notice of this warning can only mean that consciously, fully aware of the responsibility they were assuming, and of the consequences of their action, they deserted the principles they themselves had forced the international Communist movement to accept in the past. They simply threw the Communist parties overboard as so much ballast. During the period when the Soviet Union was isolated, proletarian internationalism was of enormous help to the first Socialist country in the world. Now the Soviet Union felt strong and self-sufficient enough to get rid of something that hindered her actions in some way. The Soviet Union not only went against the principles of proletarian internationalism, but she also broke with them entirely. This is the end of affection and solidarity; if you do not want to go along with us, you can go to hell. We couldn't care less.

The end of this demand for discipline may seem undesirable today, but in the end it will be all to the good. Communists have been relieved of the necessity of furthering Soviet policies and can at last work out their own policy in conformity with the interests of their own people and no one else.

In 1948, when the stern men of our Party came to power, Moscow centralism was still strict. Tito did not submit, and was cursed and excommunicated. The apparently tragic fate of Tito and his Socialist country made a profound impression on the other Communist parties. Gottwald could not have become a second Tito, nor did he aspire to. For one thing, unlike Yugoslavia, which had held out against the Nazis and defeated them with her own strength, Czechoslovakia had been liberated by the Red Army. For another thing, according to secret clauses in the Yalta Agreement, which were not at that time public knowledge, Czechoslovakia belonged to the Soviet sphere of interest. And then there was Gottwald's own gratitude to Stalin for pardoning his mistake at the time of Munich. At the beginning of the fifties, Stalin must have presented him with a terrible bill for this pardon. He asked for no more and no less than the heads of Gottwald's friends, the men he had worked with for years, the "lads from Karlín" with whom he had come to power in the Party in 1929.

It is well known that Gottwald held out for a long time. But in the end he signed, he signed the death warrants. He gave his comrades up to the executioner. Did he realize that this marked his own end? That after the Slánsky trial his only refuge would be drink, and that drink would soon take him to the grave? Maybe he knew. He always enjoyed a drink, but in those few months he drank himself to death. The people, unaware of all the web of horror, were weeping as they followed him on his last journey. Then his name fell into oblivion for a long time. If it did crop up in the papers or in historical studies, it was mentioned in connection with the monstrous deformation of Party and public life, in connection with his personal share of the responsibility for the terrible, unforgivable and irrevocable crimes committed in the name of Socialism, in the name of the Party. The Slánsky trial brought down in ruins the whole of Gottwald's past, his concept, his power. He crashed, as his antagonist Beneš had done a few years before.

February, 1948, released a surge of contentment, enthusiasm and initiative throughout the nation. At last we were going to run our own affairs, at last the people were masters, nobody would be able to exploit the common effort for their own ends, nobody would be able to deceive us, sell us to our enemies, betray us. All we had to do now was to build up our Socialist country to be a little paradise on earth, a secure paradise because the root of all social evil had been dug out; we were all going to be good, moral, and united, and our road to a joyous future would be more like a Sunday-afternoon walk than like day-to-day drudgery; there would be nobody to rob us of the well-earned fruits of our labors. Equality, freedom, and the prospect of a happy future . . .

We all fell victims to this illusion in those months. True, the remnants of the defeated class were still with us. They would never reconcile themselves to the loss of their social and economic positions, their carefree, exploiting, pleasure-filled life, their profits. They would try intriguing, splitting, sabotage— they were subtle, capable of disguising their true intentions beneath a mask of loyalty and enthusiasm. Beware of these people! They are still dangerous! Let the hard fist of the revolution crush them! Later on we may be able to take risks, but we cannot afford to be too generous yet. We have left them their lives, they are free citizens; if they had won we'd have been shot. They had better behave properly, modestly, and start doing an honest day's work . . . or else. . . .

The revolution, like any other social order, needs its executive organs. On the initiative of Slánsky and with the consent of the Party leadership as a whole, a new security body was created within the Ministry for the Interior, with the single task of tracking down, rendering harmless and destroying all the enemies of the Socialist order. In the Executive Committee of the Party it was Slánsky himself who took charge of this body.

It soon appeared that things were not going as well as we in our naïveté had thought they were. In industry, in supplies for the consumer market, in the intricacies of political, economic, cultural and social life, there was something wrong now here, now there; things limped along or got stuck in blind alleys. The reason was always very simple: them! They were still with us! They were sabotaging, confusing the situation, destroying the work of our hands in a subtle way. They had not died out when they were defeated, far from it; they were here and they were everywhere. We had to hit back even harder. Harder! Harder!

It was easy to point to "them"—members of the defeated bourgeoisie and their spokesmen among the intellectuals. They would not have dared do anything on their own, though; they had friends to help them, well-hidden and invisible as often as not. The Trotskyites, the right-wing Social Democrats whose membership in the Communist Party was only formal, and who after the fusion of the two left-wing parties, the Communist and Social Democrat, had never relaxed their traditional hatred of Communism. And all the deviationists. The Trotskyites! A dangerous element, how dangerous could be seen from the Moscow trials in the thirties. Did not Stalin teach that in the sharpening class struggle the class enemy mobilizes all its ideological reserves? Beware, beware! We shall be safest if we put them all behind bars. Then there are others—those who spent the years of exile in the West, including, alas, many Communists, infected by the poison of the Western way of life, paying undue admiration to degenerate Western culture. They do not believe in the creative power of Socialism! Beware, beware! We shall be safest if we remove them from posts where they could harm us.

Then there are the bourgeois nationalists, Party members often highly placed, but inclined to nationalist deviations which they put above the class interests of society. And since, as Stalin taught us, every coin has two sides to it, and a right deviation brings a left deviation in its wake and vice versa, there are the cosmopolitans, men who have never sympathized with the working class and the people, men without a country, international adventurers who are sinisterly clever at masking their true thoughts. There is the most dangerous offshoot of all, the Zionists! They are a mortal danger to the international Communist movement, and to Czechoslovakia in particular, for here they are at the very heart and brain center of the Party.

This hysterical witch-hunt, constantly growing, was intended to allow inefficient politicians to cast the blame for their inefficiency on others (for what ruler in history has ever confessed that he did not know how to rule, that he was not fit to rule, that he had failed those who had placed their hopes in him?). It culminated in a terrible speech by Klement Gottwald in which he threw suspicion on the volunteers who had gone to fight in the Spanish Civil War. In his opinion, since most of them had passed through the hands of the Gestapo and not been able to stand up to its torture, becoming the tools of their torturers, these men had lost the confidence of the Party. Thus step by step everybody who had done more for the victory of Socialism, for the victory over Fascism, was purged. In some way these people were outstanding. Beware of them! Only Stalin can be outstanding in the day of the personality cult—no one else, not even Gottwald.

The purges were carried out very thoroughly; those who had fought in the West were removed, as well as those who had fought in the East. In the course of questioning, the words were often heard: Comrade, how do you explain the fact that you survived the concentration camp when so many died there? In the end the hard fist of the revolution was beating up the working class. Were you a partisan? One whose name was a legend, not just an ordinary rank-and-file partisan? Away with you. You fought in the East? Away with you. You were an officer in the Rising? Away with you. Before the Rising you served the Slovak State. When I was editor in chief of *Kulturný Život,* for years I used to get together the former officers of the Slovak National Rising for consultation. I would address them:

"Comrades in the ranks, Colonel and General . . ."

Fourteen of them were left. Seven out of eight generals were demoted to the ranks. Four colonels demoted to the ranks. Of two lieutenant colonels one was degraded to the ranks and one to the rank of captain.

I asked them whether they would do the same again, after what they had gone through since; only one said he'd think twice about it.

People like that were treated like dirt. Who treated them like dirt? Who humiliated them, imprisoned them, tortured them? On what grounds were they "convicted" of sabotage and subversive activity against Socialism? The state security police, the all-powerful secret police, used as its spies pathological professional informers and also men chosen from among the victims and given a doubtful freedom in return for their services; they used, too, proscribed Fascist thugs who had no other alternative but to serve. Thus the "mailed fist of the working class" took the form of this shady and often pathological underground force whose powers were almost above those of the Party and the government itself and which became the greatest single power in the state, unchecked by any hand, even that of those who had established it in the first place, and whose responsibility it was to direct it. The Republic was a Socialist one, but it was ruled by the fifth estate; the loyalest citizen of all was—the professional informer.

The atmosphere grew unbearable. Every day at that time I was meeting Ján Rozner—one of our finest literary critics and political writers. We walked up and down Palisade Street in Bratislava, talking about it all, about what we had noticed, about our doubts, about Stalin, about the terror. Walking about was better than sitting down anywhere; when we saw a shadow we would fall silent until it had passed and was far enough away. It was a magnificent feeling of confidence in one another in those dark days—with one reservation. Whenever he, or I, wanted to say something that had a whiff of the gallows about it, we commented heretically: it's a risk, you may be in their pay, but I'll risk it anyway.

Those were the days when three drinks in a public bar might be enough; you only had to say jokingly that you were "going to get 'em," anybody, nobody in particular, anybody they cared to imagine; it was enough to dial the security police and give a secret, anonymous tip. Before long the unsuspecting sleeping citizen found himself confessing that he was in touch with the American spy Field, the Tito spy Siracký and that he had given the French Deuxième Bureau detailed plans of the jam factory where he worked in the accounts department.

For according to Andrei Vyshinsky's legal theory, the confession of the accused was the main evidence, the evidence to crown all evidence, valid even where there was no other evidence, valid even if it contradicted all the other evidence. And when more than one prisoner objected to the way his questioners tried to get a confession out of him, saying it reminded him of what he had suffered at the hands of the Gestapo, they laughed at him. The Gestapo? Mere amateurs!

We wanted to try it out. When all the possible treasonable and deviational isms had been laid bare, Rozner and I thought up one that had not yet been discovered: "Viliamism." We spread it around and waited to see how soon it would get back to us. It was back in four days, in a form that took us by surprise.

"It's Široký now, things look bad for him."

We had not thought of that. When we thought up the new deviation and tried to find a name for it, we were thinking of William Shakespeare, and didn't stop to think that Široký's first name was Viliam.

It was as easy as that.

The Czech people still remembered the painful years of a different terror, that of Nazism, more easily than the Slovaks. Terror is terror, whoever threatens whomsoever with it; terror has its own forms, its ways and means, its visible and invisible consequences. Its aims have always been the same, from ancient times to our own day: to terrify the people, spread an atmosphere of distrust, to ravish the free mind of man. A ruling power can gain respect and authority among the people by its wise acts, convincing them that it is acting in their interests. In such a case authority is identical with popularity. What if a ruling power is not capable of that, does not know how to rule, does not know how to solve the problems that are behind the thoughts and actions of the people? When they cannot get results however hard they try, when nothing goes right? What if those in power ought to depart and let others take their place, better equipped to rule, better able to rule? Will they do it? Will those whom the nation has just declared victors and given them complete confidence dare to do it? Are they morally strong enough to say: "We have done what we were called upon to do, and achieved for you what we wanted to give you. We thought we would carry on and cope with the new tasks ahead, but now we see we are not fit. We are departing in order that others, better qualified to rule than we, may take our place."

Maybe it has happened, in other ages and other countries, but it did not happen in Czechoslovakia. They stayed put and tried to throw the blame on others, on a widening circle of other people. When confidence in them began to recede, they began to strengthen their position by the use of force. Where trust is lacking, General Fear is in command. Every evening you'll have a bag ready by the door, with the bare essentials, for you never know, you can't tell, when your hour will come, and the doorbell will ring. If you do not feel at all guilty, so much the worse for you. For as you enter that dreaded building in February Street your eyes meet a long banner across the wall with the words: "Every man is a potential enemy, and it is your duty to expose the enemy and render him harmless."

In an atmosphere where every man is a potential enemy, every man becomes one in time.

The consequences were disastrous. Soon in the name of ideological purity, unity of principles, class struggle and patriotic emotion so reminiscent of the Nazis, the prisons were filled with the elite of the Communist Party. Partisans. Political prisoners from the Nazi concentration camps. Volunteers from the Spanish war. Pilots who served with the RAF during the Second World War. Pilots who served on the Eastern Front during that war. Officers of the Czechoslovak Army in the West, officers of the Czechoslovak Army in the East. Commanders from the Rising. Members of the illegal Party committees under the occupation. First secretaries of the regional committees of the Party. The "seconds-in-command" from Party offices and from government departments. Members of the Executive Committee of the Czechoslovak Communist Party. Members of the Executive Committee of the Slovak Communist Party. Artists, journalists, scientists. Writers and actors. Inventors and economists. Managers and general managers from national enterprises. Ministers and their vice-ministers. All of them—Communists.

In Ruzyně Prison, Pankrác Prison, Leopoldov Prison, they were all in the same boat, guilty or innocent. Age-long political rivals carried on with their old arguments. Guilty and innocent spokesmen of the bourgeoisie grinned maliciously at them. The Minister of the Interior, the commander of the Hlinka Guard, the Jew-baiter Alexander Mach—in the yard of Leopoldov Prison he came up against General Rašla, who had led the prosecution at Mach's trial. Serves us all right, he says. . . . And Rudolf Slánsky will find himself in the dock with Communists he himself had helped to "expose," men he himself had destroyed. He will be astonished to learn—but he will confess it —that he had been hand in glove with them in his conspiracy against the Socialist Republic.

Not all of them will survive, but later on I shall talk to them, to almost all of them. It will amaze me and send shivers down my spine to find that nothing has broken their belief and conviction, that they are still Communists, that "in there" they grew wiser and more human, that nothing broke them, nothing shattered their faith.

Of each I shall ask the same question, deliberately and openly: "Why did you confess? Why did you testify that your friends had committed crimes they never could have committed, and why did they testify the same of you?"

In every case the answer was logical and understandable. Yet no two were the same. They "worked" every man over differently, and with terrible accuracy and forethought they found the weak spot in each of them; then they went at that spot until their victim broke down.

The Third

"Citizens! Friends! Brothers! The occupation armies of the five Warsaw Pact countries are looking for excuses to create incidents. Take no notice of them. Do not argue with them. Do not give them any opportunity to shoot. Don't waste a single life. Keep calm and reasonable. Go about your daily life as if they were not here. Life must not be brought to a standstill. We must not add to the damage they have done us by their occupation of the country!"

"Citizens, unite behind the legal leaders of the country, stand by Dubček, Svoboda, Černík and Smrkovský! Put up slogans everywhere that stress our unshakable unity."

"Citizens, friends, brothers, do not put up or call out the demand for neutrality. The occupation forces could use it to prove that we were trying to break away from the Warsaw Pact. Be wise, courageous, peaceful and determined. Trust us, we trust you."

"Citizens! [Viliam] Šalgovič's secret police have got lists of people they are out to arrest with the help of advisers from the occupying forces. Do not let them get any of those endangered. Help them to hide!"

"Calling Emil Zatopek! Calling Emil Zatopek! Emil Zatopek must not go back to his apartment. Emil Zatopek must not go back to his apartment. If anyone hearing this can get in touch with him, this warning should be passed on to him."

"Calling all railwaymen! Calling all railwaymen! A freight train is approaching Prague from Chocne, carrying radio location equipment to be used in locating our transmitters and jamming our broadcasts. Railwaymen, you know what you have to do!"

"Calling all delegates to the Fourteenth Extraordinary Congress of the Communist Party of Czechoslovakia. Delegates to the Fourteenth Party Congress, attention, please! Get to Prague by whatever means you can. Get to Prague, using whatever form of transport you can find. Be prepared. The Fourteenth Extraordinary Congress of the Party is going to meet soon."

"Calling delegates to the Fourteenth Extraordinary Congress of the Communist Party of Czechoslovakia! Calling delegates to the Fourteenth Party Congress! Report to the offices of the City Committee of the Party."

"Calling all delegates to the Fourteenth Party Congress! Calling all delegates to the Fourteenth Party Congress! Attention, here is an important announcement: do not report to the City Committee. Do not report to the City Committee of the Party. This is a trap. Report to the Party branches of the big factories in Prague."

"Citizens! Friends! Brothers! the soldiers of the occupation armies are hungry and thirsty. Do not let them have a drop of water! Do not give them a drop of water!"

"Citizens! Dear listeners! Do not listen to the Vltava broadcasting station! Do not listen to the Vltava broadcasting station! This station serves the occupation armies. Listen to our broadcasts, you will recognize our voices. This is the free, legal Czechoslovak radio speaking! Trust us, we trust you!"

"Calling the Czechoslovak Army commands, calling the Czechoslovak Army commands! Put your transmitters and radio location equipment at the disposal of the free, legal Czechoslovak radio! We need your help!"

"Citizens, friends, brothers! Up to now the occupation forces have not succeeded in setting up a quisling government. They are still unable to give the name of a single one of those they say invited foreign armies to help them crush the counterrevolution. There are no such names! None of our legal Party or government organs asked the occupation for any help whatsoever! We stand behind Dubček, Svoboda, Černík and Smrkovský, to a man! Be determined, be loyal, be reasonable, be peaceful. Do not let them provoke you. Listen to our broadcasts. We are with you, stand by us."

A strange thing had happened. Something no one could have counted on, something no one could have expected. The Russians had come. Together with their henchmen they had crossed the frontiers of Czecholovakia like thieves in the night. In a few hours they had occupied the whole country and divided it into ten zones, from north to south. They had brought help nobody wanted. They had come "in obedience to the call of internationalism" that nobody had signed. They had come to crush a counterrevolution that did not exist. Over six hundred thousand of them had come, one armed soldier to every twenty of us.

Thousands of tanks and armored cars, thousands of political and security advisers, a full twelve divisions up to muster, had all poured over the frontiers of an independent state, in order not to interfere in the internal affairs of that state. This noninterference started off with the arrest of the leading Party, government and other constitutional representatives of that sovereign state, who were dragged off, handcuffed, to Moscow. This noninterference continued with the surrounding of the seat of the President, Prague Castle, the seat of the head of the state whose internal affairs they had come not to interfere in. This noninterference continued with the occupation of all government department offices, all state and cultural institutions, the complete paralysis of all air transport, the partial paralysis of rail and road transport, control of the banks, radio, television; paralysis of all social, cultural and economic life, martial law during the hours of darkness, tanks destroying the crops in the fields, destroying roads and pavements, firing at innocent, unarmed citizens. This interference would be "justified" as internationalist aid to their class brothers. That was how they would put it to their own people, and they would also be so idiotic as to scatter in the streets of Czechoslovakia pamphlets purporting to be legal newspapers, giving this same argument. In broadcasts from the Vltava station a woman's voice speaking Slovak with a strong Russian accent and a man's voice speaking Czech with a marked German accent would try to convince the Czech and Slovak people that they had given an enthusiastic welcome to invaders they hated, that they fully understood what was still completely quite incomprehensible. This station, broadcasting from somewhere in the vicinity of Dresden, would declare that the free, legal broadcasts of the Czechoslovak radio were being transmitted by West German and Austrian stations.

Never in similar circumstances have so many lies and untruths, so many imbecile inventions, which not even the famous Yelochka Shchukinová would have believed, streamed out from one transmitter. The lies put out by Soviet propaganda attained astronautical proportions. Even the official lie invented by half-witted Russian propagandists in their newspapers and broadcasts. Soviet television impudently showed the world President Svoboda exchanging hearty greetings with Premier Aleksei Kosygin at Moscow airport—and was caught in a disgusting, stupid, characteristic lie. All the European television programs would be transmitting the shot with the comment that it was obviously a forgery since that fraternal, hearty greeting had been exchanged almost two weeks earlier, on the occasion of the Bratislava meeting.

A lapse? Never mind. They would keep on grinding out their story, surpassing even the great master of the art, Josef Goebbels, who put forward the well-known theory that a lie repeated a hundred times becomes the truth. They would not even bother; they just churned it out whether anybody believed them or not.

The Russians had become what they always feared most: ridiculous and foolish. It was not the first time that they had trampled underfoot the principles they themselves most vehemently insisted on in international relations, but this time they had trampled so thoroughly that no grass will ever grow there again.

To give their actions a tinge of "internationalist duty," they ordered the obedient governments of East Germany, Hungary, Poland and Bulgaria to take part in this peculiar noninterference, to take upon themselves a share of this load of disgrace and shame. With the Soviet troops came German, Hungarian and Polish troops, armies that had taken part in the rape of Czechoslovakia thirty years before. Nor is that the most ridiculous aspect of this occupation: the most ridiculous of all is that in Poland, Hungary and East Germany the whole people hate the

Russians. In this country, among our people, they possessed their only real, sincere and loyal friends, except for the pathetic Bulgarians. They could rely on the people of Czechoslovakia, but not on the Poles, the Hungarians or the Germans. The idea of Socialism was deeply rooted in Czechoslovakia, so deeply that not even the "Socialist occupation" of our country could destroy it. The future will show whether this is so elsewhere.

The occupation came at a time when the Communist Party of Czechoslovakia enjoyed such complete confidence as has never been seen anywhere else. Today, under the conditions imposed by occupation, thousands of young people are joining the Party, students and young working people. This is in sharp contrast to the unpopularity of the Communist parties (not of Socialism itself) in Poland, Hungary and East Germany, as well as in the Soviet Union. Or was it for this very reason that they came? Maybe no nation should be allowed to realize Socialism as Marx and Lenin imagined it? Maybe it was consistent Leninist democracy that shocked the fossilized Party bureaucrats in Moscow, Warsaw and Berlin? Who would dare to go further than the Soviet Union?

Something about this occupation did not work out properly, and there is something wrong with the occupation itself. Yesterday it looked as though one great illusion had been destroyed, and I, too, felt that mood of depression; but on the second day things did not look so hopeless. Nobody had joined the ranks of the occupation forces, not a single leading politician, not a single well-known person. Before long the men whom the nation suspected of potential collaboration, and on whose help Moscow had certainly counted, would give solemn and public assurance that they had done nothing against the interests of their people, that they had not deserted at the fateful moment, that they were fully behind the policy of Dubček. The weeks would pass and the Soviet Union would have found no quislings. Not one. They would have to look on helplessly while "their" Šalgovič was removed; they would be isolated, not Dubček.

Certainly rumor was doing its work; but wherever one speaker "almost certainly" proved that so-and-so was a traitor, because he was a conservative supporter of Novotný, another would be found to interrupt: Don't judge people by what they were; now you can judge by only what they are, how they have turned out now. If the Soviet Union finds any collaborators at all, so-and-so won't be one of them.

Walking about the streets of Bratislava the second day of the occupation, watching the young people demonstrating in protest, reading the slogans and posters telling the invaders to go back where they came from, observing the fantastic unity of the whole people, you cannot fail to admire the wit, ingenuity, wisdom and courage of this nation, you cannot but be carried away by its mood. Did it seem, yesterday morning, soon after they had come, that all was lost? No, it was not so, and if a miracle were to happen, the hopeful word heard everywhere, it would not be so.

You ask: the Russians in the Kremlin did not know this? Only a few days earlier I had published an article in *Kulturný Život*: an Open Letter to an unnamed ambassador of an unnamed country. I asked a question—the Russian nation, dependent on incomplete, insufficient and biased information, need not know what things are really like in our country, what we really want to do. If anyone knows and must know, because he is on the spot and is paid to know, it is the leading diplomat of a friendly country from whom our government and our people have nothing to hide. He must know and he does know. What sort of information has he been sending back home? The truth, or what he would like to be the truth?

Did they know? Did they not know? Did they commit an international crime because they were taken in by someone who gave them false information? Or was it their own wish to be informed thus and in no other way? I remembered a diplomatic incident that had been made public in Israel after the six days' war last year. Shortly before the war broke out, the Soviet ambassador, Chuvakhin, asked for an audience with Premier Levi Eshkol, in the course of which he informed the Premier that the Soviet Government was protesting the concentration of two Israeli panzer divisions on the Syrian border. Eshkol, who later recounted the incident himself, invited the ambassador to drive out with him and see for himself whether the statement was true. Israel is a small country, so small that it is practically impossible to keep anything secret. Two panzer divisions on the Syrian border, which is not even thirteen miles long, would be visible far and wide. All along the Syrian border the territory of Israel is on the slopes of the Jordan valley, so narrow that you can see absolutely everything from any point above the valley.

Chuvakhin refused the invitation with the words:

"I know best what is there and what is not."

Chuvakhin must have known all along that what he said was utter nonsense. Concentrations of Israeli troops follow a different plan which is familiar to the whole world. Israel does not need to concentrate tanks at a point which is so easy to observe. In the course of one hour, her tanks can reach any point of the Israeli frontier. From this point of view, of course, the very existence of tank units could be considered a "concentration on the Syrian border."

Were they taken in, then?

It is difficult to answer that question. The occupying forces were not provided with a supply echelon; the tanks advanced in enormous numbers but without a single field kitchen. The exhausted tank crews we had seen asleep in their seats were hungrily eating their emergency rations from the tin. Had the Soviet command actually relied on the "grateful population" welcoming their liberators as in 1945, on their being taken home and fed with goose fat and brandy? Or was this just part of the general plan? Hungry and thirsty, nervous, were they to loot and then to fire on the people who would naturally try to prevent it? However angry the reporters from *Pravda* and *Izvestia* may feel about it, the slogan calling on the people not to let the invaders have a drop of water is no proof of armed counterrevolution. For proof there would have to be cities damaged by fighting, as Budapest was . . . Prague, say, or Bratislava . . . In the end they did fire, fire wildly, justifying it by the tale that "someone had fired at them from a church tower." It could have happened, of course, in isolated cases. But even if it did, an isolated sharpshooter is no proof of armed counterrevolution. They had to invent the evidence, and anything would serve. They disarmed several units of the workers' militia and called their weapons counterrevolutionary arms dumps. A few weeks earlier there had been a rush of sympathy throughout the Soviet Union for the armed workers' militia in Czechoslovakia, the iron fist of the working class, which the counterrevolutionaries were allegedly trying to abolish.

The military occupation of Czechoslovakia was a successful operation, from the military point of view even very successful. But nothing else went according to plan. Nobody welcomed them, nobody joined them, nobody betrayed his country. They had to bring in motorized water tanks and field kitchens from neighboring countries. Nobody gave their soldiers a crust of bread or a drop of water, although they pitied them. They were forced to steal potatoes and corncobs from the fields under cover of darkness and sentries.

Czechoslovakia presented a bizarre and fantastic picture during those days. Tanks thundered down the streets, ruining the road surface and the streetcar lines, and hardly had the noise died away than workers came along to repair the streets and lay new lines. The groups around the tanks became smaller; people went about their daily tasks and took no notice of them, ignoring their presence. If a naïve young girl smiled at a shy attempt at flirtation, there would be a group of youths surrounding her, quietly taking her around the nearest corner and cutting her hair off. More proof of "counterrevolutionary terror" for the Soviet propaganda machine!

The peaceful, self-assured and dignified attitude of the people could not fail to affect the confused young soldiers. They were to have brought demoralization with them in their tanks, but here they were being demoralized themselves. In the first week the Soviet command was forced to replace some of the occupation units and bring in "fresh forces" who had not witnessed the beginning of the occupation, and who could be shown the swastikas painted on the walls as a proof of counterrevolution.

"Look, revanchists at work!"

An hour later the swastikas had disappeared.

There was no need for the radio to send out the call, people thought of it themselves. All the signposts, street names and name cards on apartment doors disappeared overnight. All the streets were called Dubček or Svoboda Street, all the towns and villages were named Dubčekov or Svobodov. At first people destroyed the signposts, but after the radio had pointed out that this was doing unnecessary damage, they simply painted them over.

In the Kladno district, cleverly arranged signposts sent a Polish unit, advancing into Czechoslovakia, back into Poland by another route. If the humorous ideas of these days could ever be collected and published, the book might well become the world's best seller.

"Gorod prevyeren, konterrevolyutsii nyet!"—"city searched, no counterrevolution!"—was the witty popular paraphrase of the Russian words written twenty-four years ago as the sappers cleared building after building of German mines: *"Dom prevyeren, min nyet."*—"Building searched, no mines."

Two days of occupation had gone by, and these words were there to meet the occupation forces at every frontier crossing, at the entrance to every town and village. That night on a tall building in a certain town the neon lights went on:

"Chekhoslovakya prevyerena, konterrevolyutsii nyet!"— "Czechoslovakia searched, no counterrevolution!"

The tanks turned their guns on the neon lights and shot them to bits.

The leading statesmen had been kidnapped and carried off, and there were fears for their lives. The banks stopped paying out money. Contact with other countries was broken off. The Post Office could not deliver. The international telephone exchanges were mute. The Russians had brought in thirty Russian telephone girls to keep an eye on the Bratislava city phone, still not functioning to full capacity. The landing strips at all the airports were occupied by military aircraft. Trains were running irregularly, and only on local lines. Prague was cut off from

Slovakia, and Russian patrols on the roads checked all cars that passed. Practically all the radio and television transmitters had been taken over. Government offices and Party secretariat offices were cordoned off. The Czechoslovak Army was surrounded at its stations; the men were not disarmed, but the barracks were surrounded by strong tank detachments. It was clear what they were aiming at, since their original intention had failed: they wanted to paralyze life completely.

It would have been paralyzed in their country, in conditions governed by bureaucratic centralism. No orders? How can we do anything, with no orders? Who would dare, with no orders?

A year earlier everything would have slowed down to a stop in Czechoslovakia, too. Six months of freedom from bureaucratic dictatorship had done wonders, set free individual initiative. Everybody knew what to do next. The First Secretary of the Party had been kidnapped and carried off to Moscow, but the Extraordinary Congress was inaugurated, and went on with its work as if Dubček had been there.

The Prime Minister was a prisoner, but the government met and discussed concrete measures to be taken in order to maintain a normal supply situation, continued production, public services.

Because of the "pressure of other business," the Chairman of the National Assembly could not come to its meetings, but the Assembly passed bills confirming the legal validity of constitutional bodies. The National Assembly, only a year earlier, was the weakest point in the political life of the country, incapable of any initiative whatsoever. It was not a new, transformed Assembly; they were still the same "old" deputies.

The whole nation was immediately informed and began carrying out the decisions of the government, the National Assembly, and the Party leadership.

This was something that led our people to regard the occupation as something that had gone wrong, not been properly worked out, a silly business all together.

"They're not even any good at occupying us—they don't even know what's going on!"

They had forgotten the radio, you see. Of course they had

occupied most of the studios. Of course, during the first day of the occupation, everybody was grateful for every minute in which we could still hear the well-known, familiar voices of our leading commentators. They did not even believe, themselves, that they would be able to go on for long.

"We do not know how long we shall be able to broadcast. You will know when we have been silenced. If you hear a new, unknown voice on this station, whatever it says, do not believe it."

Improvised broadcasting studios sprang up, serving the legal Czechoslovak radio, on the edges of forests, on islands in the Danube, in camouflaged trucks. There was a center somewhere in Moravia directing and synchronizing all the transmitters. In a few days the original three had increased to thirteen. If the radio was silent for a short time, the spirits of the people, public morale, fell.

Where are those brave announcers? Are they still alive?

In the whole of the first week the Russians only managed to knock out one transmitter, and for that they needed tank guns.

These transmitters would not stop working until normal broadcasting conditions were restored for what, alas, would already be a censored radio service.

More than once a broadcast had to be interrupted: "We have to go off the air for the time being. They have found us, we shall have to move on, they are getting nearer. . . ." Would their voices come on the air again? Every time they turned up again. . . .

In the West they called this the "radio war." Broadcasting as a weapon against tanks.

The occupation forces did not even succeed in silencing the television studios. From time to time the radio announced the next television broadcast, and the channel. They were helpless against this "radio war"; they never managed to find out where the center was, the center that organized these broadcasts.

Today it is no longer a secret. The Czechoslovak Army put its transmitters at the disposal of the legal Czechoslovak radio. They had originally been intended for quite a different purpose: as part of a well-thought-out plan, which (as we have seen) functioned excellently, and which was set up in case of war with the West taking place on Czechoslovak territory. Our expensive army was not wholly in vain; it paid dividends in the end.

Only with this help could the moral strength of the nation have been so effectively mobilized.

The occupation forces attempted to prove that the Dubček Party leadership was a minority that had no right to speak for the whole of the Communist Party. The free radio broadcast the standpoint of all the regional and district Party committees: to a man they were behind Dubček and his group. Even district committees where the leading officials were assumed to be Novotný's supporters added their weight.

The Russians declared that their army had invaded Czechoslovakia on the invitation of unnamed government and Party leaders. The radio answered with the stand taken by the government, the trade unions, and the Party Executive Committee, and above all that of the National Assembly, which, as the supreme legislative body in the country, decidedly stated that foreign armies had not been invited by any constitutional body. The Soviet Union does not seem to have realized then, nor to have realized as yet, that she had lost the political struggle implied by the invasion; the documentary records of these statements will remain, and will remain valid, whatever may happen afterward. Whatever appearance of legality the Russians wanted to create for their doubtful invasion, they should never have allowed the legally elected, valid National Assembly to take a stand on the subject. At that moment their "class aid" was exposed to the whole world for what it was: sheer aggression, in order to ravish and occupy an independent, sovereign state. The record of this will play an important role in the future. It will be laid before the Soviet Union whenever she tries to declare to the world that she respects the principle of noninterference in the internal affairs of sovereign states. It forms a precedent. She need not let it bother her now, but the time will come when it will be of vital significance for her.

The radio gave very open and truthful information on all that went on; the radio organized industrial production; the radio determined the people's moods. Everything that the radio broadcast, whether it was a call or a warning, had immediate and practical results. It was thanks to the radio that there were no serious clashes between the Soviet tanks and our unarmed young people, clashes that Soviet propagandists could have used as proof of "counterrevolution." Naturally many people began to consider the position of our country, how far we were capable of independent existence; betrayed as we were by our allies, many people thought it would no longer be possible, or right, to remain members of the Warsaw Pact.

"The President of the Republic and the National Assembly should declare Czechoslovakia a neutral country. . . ." The slogans, resolutions and messages multiplied. It sounded tempting, for it would mean that the invading armies were on neutral territory, but from the standpoint of international law, it was an unrealizable utopia which served the Soviet propaganda machine as evidence that Czechoslovakia wanted to desert her allies and annul her solemn obligations.

"Don't press this demand, it serves their purposes," the radio urged. The posters disappeared, the calls for neutrality ceased, the resolutions were no longer brought in.

With transport and telephone, telegraph and postal communication at a standstill, stocks of raw materials were soon exhausted in the factories. The radio showed great initiative and, by passing on messages of this kind, prevented enormous damage to the national economy. It can be said that production continued, and the supply situation did not get out of hand, only thanks to the system of dispatching set up by the radio.

The Executive Committee of the central trade-union organization called for a general strike; the call went out over the radio, and the strike was 100 percent; so was the fifteen-minute token strike arranged for the following morning, when all the church bells in the country rang, all the factory sirens wailed, and motorists sounded their horns. The day afterward another noise of bells, sirens and automobile horns was organized, in support of President Svoboda's mission to Moscow.

In order to explain why they could not silence the voice of

truth and freedom in our country, the occupation forces had to use strange arguments. They had not come to interfere in the internal affairs of Czechoslovakia. How, then, could they explain the fact that they shot one broadcasting station to pieces, together with everything dead and living on the premises?

It was holiday time, and tens of thousands of Czechoslovaks were abroad; children were taken unawares in holiday camps; someone died, someone else needed a rare drug . . .

What would we all have done, during those days, without the radio?

An absurd, incredible, impossible thought occurred to me; it keeps nagging at me. Czechoslovakia is a small country, and, for the second time in its half century of existence, it has been a pawn in the hands of the Great Powers. Military defense is out of the question in view of the unusually unfavorable geopolitical and strategical position of the country. Twice the country has been occupied by foreign armies, without a fight. That may happen to any small country in the neighborhood of a large and powerful one. Since the moment when those in the Kremlin proved that like Hitler they respect international treaties and obligations only when it suits them, and that otherwise they are worthless scraps of paper, Austria cannot feel safe. The neutrality of Austria was "guaranteed," among others, by the Soviet Union. The independence of Finland, Korea, Romania, the Balkans, the whole of Europe, is in danger. Not even West Germany could stand up against that powerful threat. Following the example of her worthy partner, the United States, the Soviet Union has taken upon itself the role of world policeman. The silence maintained by the United States, and its attitude of ignoring what is going on—although in the case of Czechoslovakia it could be explained as delight at the developing conflicts between the fraternal Socialist states—in the case of Western Europe leads to a well-founded suspicion that the two Great Powers have again divided the world into spheres of interest. It may not be long before the Soviet Union declares that effective aid to Vietnam is "impracticable" because of "Chinese sabotage." I was in Vietnam shortly after the Soviet Union had stopped accusing China of "sabotaging supplies for Vietnam sent over Chinese territory . . ."

That this was a lie could be proved on the spot. There is only one narrow-gauge railroad running from China to Hanoi, and that was literally jammed with consignments of Chinese rice; there was no room for anything else. To transport anything right across the vast expanse of China, and before that right across Mongolia and part of the Soviet Union, was a slow, expensive and inefficient undertaking. But North Vietnam has the excellent port of Haiphong, where supplies could be unloaded day and night without any risk, since the Americans have not bombed the place up to the moment of writing. Great quantities of any kind of cargo could be unloaded there. When after lengthy discussion, the Soviet Union finally decided to give Vietnam full material support, she immediately dropped all talk of "Chinese sabotage." Haiphong was crammed with Soviet ships. The "Chinese sabotage" story was no more than an expression of Soviet indecision whether to provoke the Americans in Vietnam or whether it was not worth upsetting them for the sake of such a small country. Particularly since the Russians were afraid that a Vietnamese victory might increase the prestige of China.

It was in Vietnam that it first occurred to me to wonder whether the Soviet Union was playing fair with the rest of the world, or even with her own Socialist world.

In the face of a new division of spheres of interest between the two Great Powers, the small nations cannot hope to maintain peace or their own independence. The only reply to aggression by that enormous destructive force is the desperate fight of the Maccabees. Yet does not the case of Czechoslovakia show another alternative—that of moral, political, civil resistance? As long as unity on this basis continues, the Soviets will not be able to set up a quisling government. Sooner or later they will have to call things by their right names, and introduce an occupation regime and occupation laws. Not that they would be afraid to do so, or incapable of it; but it would mean that even if the world has not yet really understood the true state of affairs, the situation would then be absolutely and irrevocably clear. The rest of

Europe, if it is willing and able to unite, if it is not so far gone as to be indifferent to its own fate, can still block Soviet expansion. This has nothing to do with ideological differences; this is no longer the point, just as what the Soviet Union is doing today has nothing to do with Marxism. On the contrary, it is a contradiction of Marxism. A new, fundamental conflict in the world of today is becoming clearer and clearer—that between the freedom of small nations and the imperialism of Great Powers. The small nations of Europe have only one way to defend themselves—by uniting. For in terms of modern life, all the nations of Europe are small today.

That evening I had a nightmare feeling. It is in me, it is somewhere in us all. The Russians are here, to their shame and disgrace, but somewhere, sometime long ago, we let ourselves in for it, we put ourselves at their mercy. It was not in 1945, nor in 1948. After 1948 we still held to a relatively independent policy; we realized the limits of our independence and our opportunities, but within those limits the victorious Party followed a fairly attractive policy. It is true that in Czechoslovakia the campaign against Tito was more distasteful and attained greater proportions than anywhere else, even including the Soviet Union. "Pro-Tito elements" were the first Communists to start filling our prison cells, and in the trials of Tito agents, the first death sentences were dealt out, immediately after those inflicted in the trials of "centers of reaction" in the former bourgeois political parties.

Man is a vain creature, and inclined to attribute broader significance to chance private incidents. In 1948 the Yugoslav Embassy refused to give me a visa; this was in April, when there was as yet no hint of the campaign to come.

My chief asked me whether I'd ever had anything to do with the Yugoslavs. I hadn't, either directly or indirectly. My life had never brought me anywhere near anything that concerned Yugoslavia.

"Too bad . . ." he said, puzzled; "I would have liked to have you look around thoroughly there."

What was a young, vain, self-assured reporter to think, when the bolt from the blue revealed the deep rift between the Socialist countries and renegade Yugoslavia, but that they had been afraid to give him a visa because they did not want him to see too much with his eagle eye?

In 1949 I was in Albania. My original idea had been to get in touch with the Greek partisan command in the Pindos Mountains, but I was too late. By the time I got my Albania visa in Budapest, Van Fleet's decisive offensive had begun in Greece. It was all over before I landed at Tirana airport.

In Tirana I met Greek partisans who cursed Tito and Yugoslavia for letting American troops cross their territory to attack them in the rear. This agreed with the later story put out by the Information Bureau, in the second resolution against Tito.

This goes to show that I was by no means inclined to naïve faith in propaganda even then; but what the propagandists said often agreed with what I had seen with my own eyes. I still do not know how much truth there is in the accusation that Tito let the Americans through to attack the Greek partisans in the rear. I still think it could have happened.

The revelations of later years showed the horrors we had lived through in all their nakedness. At the time most Communists believed almost all they were expected to. Nor was there any reason not to believe, up to a certain date that varied with the individual. The Party told us the truth up to February, 1948; why should things have changed after that? In whose interests would it be to deceive the people?

And so with a greater or lesser degree of confidence, we listened to the various "revelations." I was not even surprised when the officials began to investigate my "Zionism" in 1950. The fact that they did not arrest me I put down to their confidence in me, their acceptance of my statement that I had never been a Zionist. In fact they did not accuse me outright of Zionism. They wanted to find out about the death of Folke Bernadotte in September, 1948; what did I know about the murder? They even had some right to inquire, because of a series of coincidences. A rare thing happened to me then. I described my experiences in Jerusalem with the Stern gang of terrorists; how an armed man came to see me in my hotel and told me that, in view of the corruption rife among regular government counterespionage officials, they had taken it into their own hands; and how in the course of conversation he declared that Bernadotte could come to Jerusalem, that might happen, but once he arrived he would not get away. . . .

I put the title "How Much Longer Has Bernadotte To Live?" over my article, and the issue in which it appeared carried a stop-press item: Bernadotte had been murdered in Jerusalem.

When people started telling me mysterious things about the goings-on at security headquarters, I did not believe them. They had not had anything to do with the secret police, I had, and they had been polite and decent. They had not believed my explanation, had not believed that I really knew no more about the matter than what I had written in that article, but they applied no pressure and used no threats, and when I had signed my statement they said I could go, I was free, and it was only my duty to come and tell them anything else I might happen to remember later . . . when they wanted to know more they'd let me know. That was decent of them, wasn't it? Would I have believed anybody who had told me the story I told them? Hardly.

And then something happened that forced me to wonder about the way our justice worked. I had a friend in Bratislava, Jeno F.; we'd been kids together and now he was chief of a press agency. He was a charming, fast-living, amusing rogue, and when we met we drank a lot. One day his wife came to see me, distracted.

"Jeno's disappeared. He hasn't been home for three days."

I tried to reassure her; it wasn't the first time he'd gone on a spree; when he'd had enough he'd be back.

No, no, there must be something behind it . . . she was scared, terribly scared . . . he might be . . . inside . . .

I wanted to help her, to make sure he wasn't "inside" and calm her fears. I saw no reason why he should be "inside" anyway. I promised to find out for her.

I went to see a man I had been very friendly with at the Party

School, and whom I knew to be pretty high up in security. He would be able to find out for me, discreetly, whether Jeno was "inside" or not, and if so, why.

He welcomed me warmly and brought out a bottle of plum brandy from beneath his desk.

When I told him what I had come for, he changed beyond recognition. "Why are you sticking your nose into things that don't concern you? Do you want to see the inside of a jail cell yourself?" he shouted roughly.

I left without a word. What had happened to him? Why behave like that? What did he mean by my "seeing the inside of a jail cell myself? Why? What for? I had only gone to see him to ask about a man whose wife was worried about him. I did not believe he really was "inside"; I just wanted to satisfy her that he wasn't. I wanted to find out. If her fears were well founded and he really was "inside," then I didn't know, but I supposed there was good reason. Who can tell what's going on in another man's mind? But was this step of mine, even so, a reason to threaten me with "seeing the inside of a jail cell," too? Was it a crime to care about a friend? The puffed-up toad. Still, he must be an exception; there would be others, decent fellows, in our security services. Didn't I know from my own experience that there were?

Then came the trial. . . .

First there was a prelude, a strange one; it was something that ought not to happen in a Socialist country. Toward the end of 1950 someone rang my bell about midnight. I was still up, and when I opened the door I saw two men in leather coats.

"Comrade Mňačko, you're to come to Party headquarters with us at once."

It gave me a fright. At first sight I was sure they were secret police and their "invitation" to Party headquarters a mere trick. But what could I do? I went with them. The Tatra car was really going in the direction of Party headquarters. I thought feverishly, What could have happened? There was no reason why I should be taken to headquarters anyway, and at that time of night, too. When I asked them what was going on, they did not reply.

There was a long line of cars in front of headquarters, shining black official Tatras. My chief was standing by one of them, and as I got out he called: "Come along, hurry up." I got into his car and he shouted to someone: "O.K. we can go."

We tore along through the night; I did not know where to or why. There were two others, unknown to me, in the car with us. We drove through Nitra, shot through Zvoleň, and turned south toward Lučenec. To my insistent questions the chief replied that he really didn't know any more than I did, he'd been dragged out of bed; something serious had happened somewhere, but he didn't know what. After a long silence one of the two unknown figures spoke: a miners' rebellion in Rožňava.

We passed Rimavska Sobota; I had never driven so fast before. We sped through empty sleeping towns and villages; he might be right; we were going in the direction of Rožňava.

When we got there the square was full of policemen, armed militiamen and civilians in leather coats. Our convoy drew up in front of district Party headquarters. As I got out I was amazed to see the highest Party officials in Slovakia, and some members of the regional government, getting out of the other cars. The entrance to the Party offices was protected by sandbags, and behind them were two machine gunners. There was not a window on the square showing a light, and they were all closed.

A council of war was held at once. The regional Party secretary was there, Priesol, one of the stupidest I have ever come across. All the regional officials were there. The district secretary reported on what had happened. That morning the women had been lining up for bread for hours when the manager told them, about ten, that there wasn't going to be any. They'd telephoned from Košice to say there wasn't any. The women went mad and dragged the unfortunate man about the square, beating him with sticks torn out of the fences. Then the men joined in, the miners. They marched on the district committee offices, and, when they found the doors locked, they broke them down, rushed in and demolished the furniture. The clerks who did not manage to get out the back door in time were beaten up. The afternoon shift did not go down into the mine; the miners attacked other public buildings, assisted by this time by men from the surrounding villages. The square was crammed full of people, besieging the Party headquarters, which was protected by a cordon of police and militiamen. By the afternoon the tension had reached breaking point; on the one side were armed men with rifles and machine guns, and on the other an angry crowd of miners armed with stones and lead piping and whatever they could find. One word, one shout, would have sufficed to start a fight.

That fool Priesol telephoned from Košice with orders to fire on the crowd. Fortunately the regional commander of the security service had more sense. When the men started booing the secretary, he went out to speak to them himself.

"Break it up quietly. There will be a proper investigation and those responsible will be punished. We'll get bread here in the morning. We are on your side; we belong to you. We do not want to spill the blood of the workers, and we are forbidden to. Look around you; there are machine-gun posts on the roofs. There is nothing you can do against such superior forces, and you would only cause unnecessary bloodshed. We do not want that to happen. I am giving my men the order to retire outside the town. If you still want to smash up Party headquarters, the headquarters of your own Party, then you can get on with the job. I'm not going to have the workers fired on."

That was the right way to talk. The revolt was over. The miners elected a delegation on the spot to put their troubles to the authorities. And at the far end of the square, as if in answer to their call, the yellow bread trucks suddenly appeared. The crowd slowly melted away.

The night was still tense, though; the revolt threatened to spread to other mining towns and villages.

I liked the way it had been settled without bloodshed. There had been plenty of rebellions in the history of Slovakia, but under the First Republic, there were always a few dead in the square afterward. I could not imagine the Socialist security forces firing on the workers. That never happened, anywhere.

Next morning Communist miners were called to a meeting in the local movie theater, and Karol Bacílek addressed them. He spoke off the cuff, without notes; it was a magnificent speech. I had often heard him before the war; he knew how to excite his audience, get them ready for action. But this was even more: three hundred men as hard as nails, men whose lives were spent warring with stone—there they were, sobbing like little kids. Bacílek told them to their faces the naked, bitter truth. . . .

It would happen often enough that he would deliver a dull, empty two-hour speech made up of familiar phrases; he would stumble and falter over a text he had not written himself, feverishly looking for where he had lost his place, stammering foreign words. His audience would shrug scornfully: what leaders we've got! Can't even read properly. There would be many embarrassing and evil stories told, many ridiculous moments to be got through. But I shall never forget that morning in Rožňava. Perhaps it was the last time he shone as the famous orator, the rebel, the defender of the common people. The sensitive, successful improviser.

He was never any good at desk work, and he never got any better. Everything he did at his desk was stupid, and he was responsible for many unforgivably and irredeemably damaging decisions. But he had been a great man. He could rebel, rouse others, excite the crowds, but he could not govern.

In Rožňava that day, I felt he knew his own power. This was his familiar ground: a rebellious, angry throng that he would grip with his eloquence, convince and deflect from rebellion to loyalty. He alone, the tribune of the people, the ruler of the masses. . . .

As he spoke it was clear that he would squeeze the utmost out of those miners. Instead of resisting, they would work even harder, go on even more Sunday shifts, get up even more ore. . . .

When it was all over, I heard the regional security commander say to him discreetly, but loud enough for me to catch:

"I'll have a warrant out for that Jew."

I did not understand what he was talking about, but it was strange. That Jew . . . that was a new one on me; our laws did not allow any such classification.

For a long time I could not understand why they had taken me down there with them. There was nothing I could write about the rebellion, as I had realized the moment I got out of the car in the town square. I stayed there for a week, visiting the miners' homes and going down into the mine with them. I found that the bread had only been the last straw, the grain of sand that tipped the scales. The real cause of rebellion was elsewhere, in the nationality problem in this mining area. This was a painful and unresolved question, particularly since the unsuccessful deportation of the Hungarians from this predominantly Hungarian region after the war. The underground miners are all Hungarians, while the comfortable office jobs are all held by Slovaks.

"Just go and look at the railroad station," they suggested. "You can get a better answer there, every morning, than anything we can say. Before six the workers' trains leave for the north, for the Slovak parts. You won't get far if you talk Slovak with those men. Before eight the "office workers' train" comes in from the north. You won't get a word of Hungarian out of those men, even if they understand the language."

Then came the trial. I had been in Košice for some time, writing about the big Socialist construction schemes. The Bratislava office sent me to cover the trial, giving me a whole page for it. In the corridor of the court building, I ran into Karol B., chief regional judge in Bratislava. What was he doing here?

"What do you think I'm doing? They sent me down here to hear the case. We're going to get that swine."

"This is out of your jurisdiction, isn't it?"

"That's a mere formality. Nobody bothers these days."

The fact that Judge B. was conducting the trial promised to provide a sensation. He was a friend of mine, a wonderful person off the bench, fond of good wine, good food, pretty women, and sexy stories, but on the bench he had a reputation for stern but fair decisions, a judge to whom the death sentence seemed almost the only penalty. In the courtroom I saw the accused, a pale little man with shifty eyes, a thin nose and very thin lips. This notorious "king of the millers," about whom there had been so much talk recently, sat between two warders. His appearance was not prepossessing—which of course must mean he was capable of anything. He behaved as badly as possible before the court, denying every accusation made by the prosecution, and when confronted with witnesses, simply shrugged his shoulders. Once or twice with a clear note of scorn he said, "If that's what you think . . ."

I did not see the point of the whole trial. The king of the millers, Ladislav G., managing director of the East Slovak Mills, was accused of causing serious damage to the Socialist economy of the country by:

Having his office car painted gray to suit himself, although the experts brought to testify declared that the old coat of paint was good enough.

Using the said office car more often than the official quota allowed, in order to take his boon companions to orgies in the Tatras.

Behaving arrogantly and brutally toward his subordinates, for example repeatedly saying: "Get out of my office before I kick you out on your ass."

Allowing one of the mills to become infected with worms, which was a danger to public health.

In one of the mills under his management, the security police found sixty hoes, the property of the former millowner Baroness S. This public property could not have been secreted there without the knowledge of the accused.

Allowing several tons of bread to be used for pig food on a farm in Čane, at a time when there was a shortage of bread and strict rationing was in force.

As a former capitalist, the owner of a canning factory, he had wormed his way into the Communist Party in order to abuse the trust of the workers and more easily carry out his plans to sabotage the people's democratic regime which, as a class enemy, he hated.

That was all. Little enough for a trial of these dimensions, little enough to lead them to ignore the valid system and send down the feared head judge from Bratislava. I waited for what was still to be revealed. But except for a fiery speech by the prosecution and a few confused remarks by the defense that seemed to make matters even worse, that was all—except for the sentence.

The sentence was death.

That shook me. The sentence suggested that there was more at stake than met the eye, for taken all in all the misdemeanors proved against the accused could not have been called real sabotage of the Socialist system. In the judge who was well known to me, I saw a guarantee that there was nothing wrong, in spite of appearances to the contrary, and that justice was being done. I thought of Al Capone, with many murders on his conscience, sentenced for tax frauds although everyone knew of his real crimes. They must know, including my friend the judge, that the accused was a particularly dangerous criminal who had covered up his crimes so well that he could not be charged with them, although they were well known to those with inside information. They had got him on a count they could be sure of, revealing only part of his dirty deeds. Hadn't I been in Rožňava? Didn't I know what was going on in the region? Who was responsible for that state of affairs? The bakers? They could only use what they were given. Now they had caught the real culprit. I was still willing to put the blame on individuals instead of seeking for it in the inefficient system, run by people who did not know how to govern.

I filled the entire page that had been allotted to me by my paper, with my story of the case of public enemy Ladislav G. I did not deny the flimsy nature of the proof produced, but I mentioned the case of Al Capone. I exposed the dangerous, sly creature and his treacherous methods of sabotage. Proof? What about the miners' revolt, the shortage of bread throughout the region, and the very poor quality of what bread there was?

I found the sentence extremely severe, but thought it would serve as an example. Let all criminals of this type tremble in their shoes! Let this sentence be a warning to them!

Oh, I was good at it, exposing and convincing, a good pamphleteer.

Life went on, and I had almost forgotten that trial, never dreaming that I would return to it and keep on at it for many years to come. The supreme court of appeal reduced the death sentence to one of twenty years' imprisonment, and I sighed with relief: we are stern, we are very stern indeed, but we are humane! It was enough to prove that sabotage of this degree could earn the death penalty; I was glad the sentence was not to be carried out.

I was to come back to this trial; I was to go around talking to the witnesses and learning that many of them had given their evidence under threats and said the opposite of what they would have liked to say. Six years later I managed to get Ladislav G. a conditional release, and finally to worry the Premier into granting him his freedom. I was to be one of those who had his case retried by the committee appointed to investigate cases of abuse of the law. This committee repealed both sentences and recommended that the accused, condemned to death, should be tried only for his actual misdemeanors—not crimes. He would come before the court for the third time, and be sentenced to five months' imprisonment. He would appeal against this sentence, on my advice, and be given by the Bratislava regional court a sentence of the length he had already served—seven and a half years. The court at least declared that he had already served his full time.

Then we would fight on together, until a few years later the Supreme Court declared him innocent on all counts, thus making it clear that the law had been flagrantly abused and an innocent man condemned; he would be granted damages for the years spent in jail.

Until he was released I would be a father to his son, a friend helping his wife.

And finally, I would confess my own share in all this, give public satisfaction for my contribution, as a journalist, to a dirty, evil business. But all that would come years later. . . .

Then, in those days, I did not guess it was only the first in a long series of cases of grave abuse of the law, arbitrary justice, a rule of terror instituted by those whose duty it was to see justice done and the law maintained.

As yet I did not bother much about the few remarks about Jews. The eastern end of the republic was still odd in some ways.

Soon after this trial, the judge I respected, who had given this hard sentence, asked to be relieved of his office. He was made Vice-Minister of Culture, and from time to time we met in Prague, although I did not seek him out; there were many points at which our ways met.

"Karol," I asked him every time, "what about that sentence?"

He did not turn aside, he did not avoid me as the Minister of Justice was to do later, crossing the road rather than meet me, and not even bothering to pretend he had to buy some cigarettes.

Once, not long before his death, the judge would give me an answer which was more than a guilty smile.

"Why do you keep on asking? Is it so hard to guess? They put me into a plane and gave me a dispatch case with the papers on the case and the sentence all complete."

That was a good enough explanation. It must have been that way.

The case of Ladislav G. was the first I was to come up against, where the law was abused to get rid of Communists. Soon it became the usual thing, and when I realized what was going on, in two or three years, I went back to that first case. I had a guilty feeling that I had helped in the dirty work.

I do not know now, and I shall never know, why the Party bigwigs took me down to Rožňava when the rebellion broke out, and when it was not possible to write about what happened at the time.

I do not know whether anyone at the time realized that this trial was a modest prelude to the Slánsky trial. A modest, almost insignificant prelude, but one that was already carefully thought out.

In 1948 the state of Israel came into existence. I was there the day independence was declared, and I went through almost the whole of the first Arab-Israeli war as a reporter for the Czechoslovak press; after my return I added a book to the dozens of articles I had written—my first book. Today it sounds like one of the ironies of history that the decisive factor in the creation of an independent state in the Jewish part of Palestine was the common stand of the USA and the USSR in the Security Council and the General Assembly of the United Nations in 1947, when the decision to partition Palestine was taken. It was fairly clear what interest these two powers had in the solution put forward. The United States pretended to be following the traditional American anticolonialist policy, and hoped on the side to weaken the position of Great Britain in this part of the world, so important for the oil business. The Soviet interest seemed even more straightforward: to weaken imperialism wherever possible and to involve it, whenever possible, in internal conflicts. Reading the speech made by Andrei Gromyko in the Security Council on that occasion, and comparing it with the speech he made in the summer of 1947, one can only admire with malice. How things change!

Besides these clear and obvious motives, there was a deeply rooted sentimental internationalism alive in the Communist movement. The Soviet Union wanted to deal a blow at the feudal Arab rulers; if not the Soviet Union, then at least Czechoslovakia subscribed to the illusion that Israel, dependent on the aid of the Socialist countries, could become a Socialist country. Did they not have their kibbutzim, communal organizations on a Marxist basis? If we were to send a few thousand Czechoslovak Jews out to help, most of them Communists, that should do the trick, together with our military aid.

The Soviet Union guaranteed the existence of Israel but did not directly commit herself. It is difficult to say today whether the Czechoslovak Communist Party was acting on orders from Moscow, or whether it decided to support Israel on the grounds of internationalist duty. It is even more difficult to determine today whether this support for Israel was suggested in the first place by the Jewish comrades in the Party leadership. Slánsky was well known for his fierce anti-Zionism, and the Fischl who was sentenced for Zionism alongside him was an open enemy of Jews wanting to leave Czechoslovakia. Such attitudes, however, are often only a disguise to cover the real views held.

However that may be, one thing is sure: it was Czechoslovak

arms that decided the outcome of the fighting in the Middle East, that saved the newborn state of Israel from defeat and hundreds of Jews living there from physical extinction.

In my book, as in the articles I sent home, I warned clearly against the illusion that we were supporting or inspiring Socialist progress, or even Socialism itself, in a new part of the world, a new sphere. In vain. This illusion was too well grounded in the minds of Czechoslovak Communists.

(Eight years later, after a short but extremely interesting visit to Egypt, I gave the same warning about illusions on the subject of Egyptian Socialism.) We suffered disillusionment when our hopes were not fulfilled, and when what we had so earnestly supported did not come off (not that our support was a total loss, for Czechoslovakia remained in Israel's debt after the break, since millions of dollars owed to Israel were frozen in Czechoslovakia and have still not been paid). Perhaps this disillusionment helped to strengthen the line taken later in the Party and in the state. Israel did not declare itself a Socialist republic, and thousands of Jewish Communists who left this country (after secret military instruction at the hands of the Czechoslovak Army) promptly ceased to be Communists when they got to Israel. This could have led us to doubt whether those who remained and were still members of the Party were in fact Communists or not. What I do know is that after the disappointment over Israel, anti-Semitism began to appear in the Party.

Journalists and historians in the West connect the wave of anti-Semitism that flooded the country, inspired by the highest circles, with the traditional anti-Semitism of Stalin. They point out the parallel between the Slánsky trial and the trial of the Jewish doctors in Moscow. The affair of the "cosmopolitan doctors who wanted to poison Stalin" broke out later than the beginning of anti-Zionism in Czechoslovakia. If there is any direct influence, it is more likely to be the other way around, and that events in Czechoslovakia reminded Stalin of his old aversion.

Today I know that anti-Semitism was not the goal in Czechoslovakia, and that it cannot explain anything.

The immediate preliminary to the Slánsky trial was the revelation of the "anti-Party, treasonable espionage work" of Šling, the regional Party secretary in Brno. This event was widely commented upon and led to the first wave of witch-hunting. One of the main "discoverers" of the evil doings of Šling and "his mistress Marie Švermová," head of the organizational department of the Central Committee offices of the Party, widow of the national hero Ján Šverma, who perished in the mountains during the suppression of the Slovak National Rising, was Rudolf Slánsky himself. It is hard to say now whether he was trying to distract attention from himself and deflect the catastrophe he knew was on its way. In fact the two cases, that of Šling and that of Slánsky later, need not have been connected at all, and may only have been put into the same context by later stage managers.

There are two terribly shocking documents that were published in the Czechoslovak press at the time, and that date from the revelation of anti-Party, treasonable espionage centers; they must be the most disgusting documents ever put out by the Communist Party. Both were delivered before the plenary session of the Central Committee of the Party by the chairman of the committees set up to investigate the two cases, Václav Kopecký, of the Executive Committee—the worst of the evil spirits behind the Party machine, a revolting, pathologically perverted megalomaniac and erotomaniac, a man of exceptionally filthy mind and deeds. I have already confessed to hating him with an inhuman hatred, but that does not mean that I exaggerate his character here. That is the kind of man he was. For years it was he who formulated the Party's cultural and ideological program. He was feared as an unprincipled demagogue who was all the more dangerous because of his oratorical ability to seize his audience's imagination. When he went into the bedroom intimacies of Šling and Švermová, which could hardly have taken place as described, he grunted in perverse satisfaction like a pig at the trough of swill. It was he, in the course of his "revelations," who introduced the term "Izzie" into the Party vocabulary.

While he presented Šling as an individual who had sold himself to the imperialist spy network, he pointed to Slánsky as the head of a treasonable, anti-Party espionage center involved with all the imperialist spy agencies.

Vladimír Clementis, one of the two non-Jewish members of this spy center, was described as having been connected with Tito and having worked as an agent of the French Deuxième Bureau. Slánsky allegedly had worked for the American CIC and Tito's spy ring, and in addition had fostered Zionist influences in the Party. Fischl was directly said to have collaborated with the Israeli secret service. And so it went on, around all fourteen accused. All of them were allegedly united in their hatred of the people's democratic regime and the Czechoslovak people and in their support for cosmopolitanism and Zionism— of which Clementis was also guilty.

I was not particularly concerned over the arrest of Šling. Kopecký proclaimed his indictment with his usual fervor, but there might be something in it after all; it would not be reasonable to suppose that the enemy would not try to upset the Party from within. But in the interval between the arrest of Slánsky and his trial, in the course of a few months, my ideas underwent a great change. At the time of the revelations about his spy ring, I believed, along with most other people, that he really had done what was attributed to him. I remembered my own experience with him; since then I had watched his career closely, and I knew that he was capable of destroying people, and the methods he used. It was he who first instituted and inspired the reign of terror; it was he who had under him the ever more powerful secret police. I knew about the arrest of Josef S., a regional Party secretary, and about his conviction and sentence. It had been said of him for a long time that he had been a Gestapo informer who had more than one death on his conscience. That could have been true, and indeed it was soon shown to be true. Slánsky could not have failed to know about the rumors, but he "took steps" only when the former Gestapo man got in his way; in fact he did not even get in his way, but simply disagreed with some measure and failed to carry it out. Slánsky called S. to

Prague and in the course of friendly remonstrance took a piece of paper out of his desk.

"Is this your signature?"

Josef S. grew pale. It was the promise he had given the Gestapo, the promise of collaboration, in return for which they had set several people free.

Josef S. was no longer a free man when he left the building.

It cannot be assumed that Slánsky had only just gotten hold of that incriminating document, or only shortly before. It is more credible that this document was the "secret" of Josef S.'s rapid promotion in the Party. Slánsky needed obedient puppets everywhere, people he had a hold over.

I knew enough about Slánsky to know that he was capable of anything, but there was something that warned me to be on my guard; this was the anti-Semitic campaign that was set in motion in connection with the trial, and that grew apace. Since it was made clear from the outset that the Jews were to blame for everything everywhere, I began to ask myself whether this was not an attempt to mask a profound but as yet invisible crisis in the Party and in society, whether this trial and the atmosphere created around it were not a mask for something much more serious going on in the country.

In spite of my experience of reporting trials, I refused to work on this one, with the considerable risk that I might have to pay for my refusal. Any reporter might consider it a mark of distinction to be given such an important assignment, and they did. When I refused, the acting editor in chief remarked sarcastically: "Of course, we all know what you are . . ." and it is worth adding that he was a Jew, the only one to remain in the editorial offices after the "purge."

I refused. I was enraged. I listened to the radio and turned it off in shame and anger as the trial was broadcast. For sheer arbitrary nonsense, lies, baseness and primitivism, it surpassed anything in the history of justice, not excluding the travesties of the Nazi courts. The notorious Freissler had attempted to maintain at least an appearance of legality and correct procedure, although he had before him men who had broken the "Law concerning the Safety of the Fuehrer." The proceedings of the Moscow trials at the end of the thirties made some sort of sense, although it is difficult for the reader to imagine a chauffeur attempting to kill Molotov in such a way that he perished himself. But things like that have happened before. During my sojourn in Budapest, I was given a ticket for the trial of Ladislav Rajk. Everything went off as it should in a court of law. The prosecution spoke against the accused, they denied their guilt, the witnesses were called and dramatic confrontations staged, and then the accused broke down and confessed. The crimes concerned were credible ones; the meeting between Rajk and Rankevitch was so convincingly reconstructed that to this day I still believe that is how it was.

There was nothing like this in the trial of Slánsky and the rest. The accused confessed their utter guilt, even going beyond what the prosecution proved against them, and accusing one another of complicity in fields in which they could not even have worked at all. I knew all the men concerned except two, and knew them from more than chance encounters. Slánsky had shouted at me to threaten me with prison, Clementis had tried to send me into the diplomatic service (that was a mania of his, to try to get young Slovak writers and journalists to become diplomats); Reicin had threatened to have me expelled from the Party because I refused to go into the army as a political worker; I had argued with Eugen Loebl in the pages of *Tvorba* and in conversation, not seeing eye to eye with him on the subject of foreign trade; at one time André Simon had wanted to "buy" from me the manuscript of my chronicle of the February crisis of 1948, which Slánsky had refused to allow me to publish. I saw Simon frequently, for we both worked on *Rudé Právo;* Frejka was also a man I saw often—he was Gottwald's chief economic adviser and head of the brain trust Gottwald gathered around him.

I had met many others who, although their names came up in the course of the trial, were still waiting for their own turn. The accused confessed their crimes, crimes about which I knew something and therefore knew that it could not have happened that way. Slánsky confessed to the murder of Ján Šverma by deliberately giving him boots two sizes too small during the retreat into the Slovak mountains, although he knew he was in a high fever. Reicin confessed to collaboration with the Gestapo and a particularly revolting piece of informing—that he had handed over to the Gestapo the national hero, Julius Fučík. This crime was attested to by Fučík's widow, Gusta, and under the weight of this evidence Reicin confessed, although I and many others knew quite well that, when Fučík was arrested, Reicin had been in the Soviet Union for over a year. Later on, running into Gusta Fučíková in Moscow, I was to ask her why she bore false witness; I did not have to press her, she burst into tears; I was not the first nor the last to ask her that, and to one of us (not me) she would reply that she was sent for and told, solemnly and convincingly, that it was in the interests of the Party for which Julius had given his life.

Slánsky, and not he alone, finally also confessed to working for foreign espionage agents even before joining the Party in the twenties, and that he joined in order to start his task of disruption when the right time came.

The Procurator-General, Urválek, seasoned these confessions and the whole course of the trial with personal insults addressed to the accused, revelations of their immorality outside their criminal activity, stressing the fact that they were Jews, that they were part of a worldwide Jewish plot, referring to their lives of luxury and the houses they lived in (and which new "stars" in the Party sky promptly inherited from them). I had a friend of many years' standing who was and remained a fundamentally decent fellow; today he is one of Dubček's standbys; he came to the fore after the trials, and, whenever we met, he would ask me around for a cup of coffee. Once I accepted, and he took me to a pleasant house in a quiet Bubeneč street, where the furniture was not what I would have expected him to have. He saw my surprise and to explain it away said: "Do you know who used to live here? Slánsky." I never went back there, and he soon came to feel that it was not a pleasant place to be and moved out.

I felt terrible. I was afraid of my own Zionist past. Ján Rozner and I went to the bars, drinking ourselves under the table. Drunk as could be, I would stop people in the street and introduce myself: I'm Mňačko, formerly Meňschell. I dreamed of a pistol and was obsessed for weeks with the picture of myself lying in front of the Central Committee building with a bullet wound in one temple. I was ashamed, ashamed of the world, and above all ashamed of myself and my own part in that ghastly, endless tragedy; I had been there, I had been one of the axes that caused the chips to fly until the trees came crashing down. I was ashamed of my Party, the Party whose two million and more members had put their hands up to vote on Slánsky's guilt and punishment; I was ashamed of myself for the fear that had seized me and made me lift my hand with the rest, calling for the death penalty. I shall never free myself of this sense of guilt and shame; I shall find myself coming back to it over and over again, coming back to the memory of those days and seeking there an explanation for my own peace of mind and for society at large. I shall be unable to let it alone, I shall be one of the first, if not the very first, to write of the need for revision of this judiciary murder and other judiciary murders. I shall write of the profound moral crisis that is one of the consequences of the trials and that cannot be solved until we tell the whole shocking and shameful truth.

I shall seek out the survivors, the widows of executed men, but in most cases they will come to me of their own accord; a man will ring my bell who has just come out of prison and say, "Forgive me, but I couldn't just pass by." He hasn't yet spoken to his wife, waiting for him at home, but he has to tell me how things were, what had happened, where it had happened; two weeks later a woman appears at my door as she comes back from "inside"; she has not yet seen her husband, who awaits her, but she could not pass by without looking in on me; a young man comes to see me, the young man who as a sixteen-year-old boy wrote a letter, printed in all the papers, in which he demanded the death sentence for his own father, an enemy of the people. Now, years later, he comes to see me and asks: "Can I go on living? How can I go on living this way?" A friend in

Prague takes me to see a woman who has written a letter that appeared in every daily, denouncing her husband and calling for the heaviest sentence for him, a sentence of death. The day after the letter was printed, two men came to see her and told her that her letter would not be taken literally, because the father-in-law of the accused, her own father, a leading figure in one of the major Communist parties of Europe, had intervened and asked for a pardon, so that one man, and one only, would escape the gallows. She was a good-looking woman, kind, clever and educated. During the evening she took a book down from its shelf and said, "There is a strange story of this sort from the Irish rebellion. The hero was condemned to death by the British and she loved him dearly, but handed him over to the firing squad because she was equally fanatical on the other side of the barricades." I would be seeing her many times after that, and she would always surprise me with something of the sort from long-forgotten literary history.

Those who survived would come out of prison and send to tell me they wanted to talk to me; and if they did not, I went to find them myself and ask for a talk with them. Later, some years later, I would publish a book called *Overdue Stories;* I refused to let it appear abroad, but at home it had an enormous response, bringing me two thousand letters a year, most of them beginning: "You wrote those stories as if you knew what had happened to me."

I become a garbage container for our shame and our sorrow; they vomit up the bitterness of their souls before me; I become a legal advice center, an office for intervention in the cause of justice, a voluntary financial aid fund, a confessor, an avenger; I shall write to the President, keeping the doors of official boards, secretariats and ministers' offices on the go, begging, threatening, proving: let this man go, read this evidence, you will see for yourself he is innocent. Sometimes I succeed, sometimes I do not. I get a visa for a foreigner who has been waiting hopelessly for his love, who is here and cannot get a passport to leave. I get it by writing openly and impudently to the President of the Republic that the man's name is Schwartz but that the President need not think he is a Jew. I get the nice but once sadistic young woman judge in a Prague civil court to abrogate three sentences she has handed down and declared valid, one of them on a certain Antonín Novotný, office worker, of Prague; I phone the rector of the university and shout at him over the phone that he's been responsible for a dirty piece of work over that student Knappo, and in a while he will phone back meekly to say that Knappo can take the exams for his medical degree whenever he wishes.

I go to see the Minister of the Interior, a new man I have never spoken to before, and tell him, "This is Mr. Minc, who was sentenced in the Oatis spy case. In view of the international complications of this affair, he has no hope of rehabilitation. He was given twenty-five years and released on probation; he cannot get a job in his own field and has to work as a furnace-man. He hates his life here; let him have a passport to emigrate." The Minister promises to look into it but points out that every passport for emigration has to go before a special commission. On our way back into town Minc sneers at my naïveté, thinking there can be any help for him once the Minister has seen the files. But two days later the Minister phones and says, "Where's that Minc you were talking about? Get him over here right away, before I change my mind! I looked at the file and it's clear he'd never get by the commission. So I've decided to let him go on my own responsibility."

I request an interview with the Prime Minister, whom I have known for many years, and ask if I can bring an old lady with me; I sit her down in front of him and say, "Look at this old soul; her son's in jail for espionage. I don't know anything about the case, but I doubt if it was one of those abuses of the law. He probably did do what he was accused of doing . . . that's not the point now. I want you to look at this poor old thing; she's got nobody in the world but him, her son, and there's such a thing as a pardon, isn't here? Not for his sake, but because of her. Look at her . . ." And he tells me signing pardons isn't his job, and I tell him I know that well enough, but that he is always meeting the people who do decide, and he promises to look into it and in a couple of days I hear from him that it's a real bad case but he'll do what he can, though I'd better not give the old lady any hope. And two months later I meet her in the street with a pale, shaven-headed man and she introduces me: "This is my Vladimír. Say 'thank you,' Vladimír," and I go on my way.

Not long ago I counted the cases I had managed to help; it came to over three hundred, of which thirty were political prisoners who had been released, or cases against innocent people that had then been dropped. This quiet work I was doing, never published anywhere except for one or two cases that I included in my *Overdue Stories,* cost me a fantastic lot of time, as well as effort and money. Even without publicity it became a saying throughout the country—if there's nobody who can help you go and see Mňačko . . . and I know of cases where it was enough to threaten bringing me in.

Over three hundred successful interventions, besides those that had no effect, is not bad, is it? I might have reason to be proud of myself.

Yet, is it so very much? Is it much when you consider that in recent months, during the discussion and passing of the law on rehabilitation of wronged victims of misrule, seventy thousand people asked for rehabilitation?

And have I anything to be proud of? To some degree, yes, for I showed that I was not indifferent to the fate of my fellowmen, wronged and persecuted. Is there anything else? That I involuntarily helped an inhuman regime to keep the semblance of humanity and justice? I remember how Minc rejoiced: so there is such a thing as justice here, after all . . . and with his passport for emigration in his pocket, he began to think of staying.

Whatever my clients thought about it, I knew very well that what I was doing for them had nothing to do with law and justice. If law and justice for any individual depends on whether a certain journalist takes up his case or not, there is something wrong, and badly wrong, with law and justice.

There is of course the other side, whether you can remain indifferent to the fate of the innocent, if you have the chance to help. But there is another thing; from the outset I was consciously and deliberately building up my own security, my own safety.

Earlier, during the time of the Slánsky trial and just afterward, when brutal terror reached its peak in Czechoslovakia, I was scared, I was dead scared, they would be coming for me; the clutches of the terror would seize me, too; and in vain did I wonder how I would behave, whether I would stand firm or be a coward—there are some things you cannot plan in advance.

For months and months I tried to drive away my own fear and panic with drink. I cannot remember exactly when it happened, but I dashed a bottle of rum to the floor and said to myself: Drink solves nothing, drink puts nothing off, drink can't protect you against anything at all. You can't live with just drink and you can't live with just fear. If fear is to be their key to control over the rest of society, let them feel it, too—let them fear you! It's the only way to stand up to it, the only way to make sure they don't get you.

It was really terribly simple. All I had to do was to understand this apparent paradox, and act accordingly.

And I realized something else as well. In any abnormal society, even an abnormal Socialist society, the best weapon and the best defense is—political scandal.

The
Fourth

The free, legal radio broadcasts were getting calmer, more thoughtful and more self-assured; the announcers no longer ended with their ominous "until you hear us again, if we can still come on the air." The whole country was covered with a well-thought-out network of transmitters, so that East Slovakian broadcasts could be heard in Western Bohemia, and vice versa. Listeners heard every important announcement several times, but nobody turned off their radios; the very fact that they were still on the air, that they were on the air at all, was an exciting experience and a spark of hope. People took their orders from the radio, following them exactly.

It was true that the news itself was bad. The President of the Republic had decided to go to Moscow for negotiations. What could he bring back with him? At best a compromise, capitulation. At this news the mood of the nation sank, sank very low, only to rise again at the news that comrades Dubček, Černík and Smrkovský would also be taking part in the negotiations—after being arrested by the Soviet Army and taken off to an unknown destination; and that the leading Slovak statesman Gustáv Husák was also there.

The radio was still issuing warnings about arrests. I did not think the arrests would begin so soon. Pavel, the new Minister of the Interior, had succeeded in a very short time in reorganizing the state police and putting new people in, men who were not compromised and who now stood by the people. The moment the report went out that so-and-so was collaborating with the Soviet occupation army and security police, the unfortunate individual concerned tried by every means to get the radio to issue a denial of the report.

I did not think the Russians themselves would go around arresting us, and it was soon clear that none of our own people would be willing to lend themselves to such a task. But I was somewhere near the top of a possible list of people in whom the Soviet forces might be interested. Friends I met in the street or at the Writers' Union were angry with me. What are you doing here? Get away!

I let myself be persuaded, and spent the third night somewhere else, outside Bratislava. I refused to go into hiding. I would not make myself too obvious, but I intended to live openly and aboveground.

It was a mistake. I took refuge in the writers' country home in Budmerice Manor, where there were several other writers and their families at the time. We were entirely dependent on the radio for our news, with no contact in the throbbing life of the city. We could only hear, but not see anything going on. I felt helpless in this isolation, just waiting, waiting to see how it would all turn out and knowing it could not turn out well. The Russians had come, and they had come to stay; there was no power that could get them out now. That was the bare truth, and it overshadowed everything else.

By the third day of the occupation, though, many things were clearer. The Soviet forces had carried out a brilliant operation and occupied Czechoslovakia so quickly and taken us so by surprise that there could be no thought of resistance; but apart from that they had succeeded in nothing at all. They had found nobody willing to cooperate with them in any way. They had not been able to announce the setting up of a government of "their" people; there was nothing but the embarrassingly stupid repetition of the idea that "true Communists" had invited them to Czechoslovakia, and the blatherings of the Vltava broadcasting station which for want of other news (a sure sign that it was nowhere on Czechslovak territory) was still sending out the ridiculous claim that the Warsaw Pact forces had come to give Czechoslovakia fraternal aid against the still inaudible and invisible counterrevolutionaries. But *konterrevolyutsii nyet,* there was no such thing; even if they tried to organize one for themselves, there would still be nothing. The Soviet Union had chosen the worst possible moment for its unheard-of, brutal act of aggression. A year earlier, when Novotný's position began to falter, there might have been plenty of people willing to come out into the streets and demand that the legal government resign. The student demonstrations were something of a prelude, and if the long-drawn-out political crisis had not been solved rapidly, Prague could have seen a repetition of Budapest.

The theory of the Hungarian counterrevolution, however, is a vulgar oversimplification. In Budapest the "most progressive force in history," the working class, fought with arms in their hands against Rákozcy and then against the Soviet Army. This was hushed up in the documents issued by all the Communist parties. True, the fighting in Budapest was a destructive battle between two different camps; it broke out as resistance to a Communist rule of terror, and Soviet forces intervened with brute force when armed groups began attacking them and killing whomever got in their way. Unlike Czechoslovakia, Hungary had Soviet troops on her territory in accordance with the terms of the peace treaty and an agreement signed between the Soviet and the Hungarian governments. There were no Soviet forces in Czechoslovakia.

Let us follow some of these points to their logical conclusion. In Czechoslovakia, let us suppose that Dubček had not replaced the bankrupt Novotný. The crisis situation was ready to explode, not in counterrevolution (that was not the point even in Budapest) but in a burst of popular indignation. In this situation suppose the Soviet forces arrived and offered to take Novotný off to the Crimea. Whom would they have relied on for their intended pacification campaign? Probably Dubček, Svoboda, Smrkovský, Černík, the very people whom they came to arrest and perhaps to destroy physically in the real situation, rather than the imaginary one. In the eyes of the Soviet politicians, Dubček, Svoboda, Smrkovský and Černík had committed the unforgivable sin of not waiting for a "second Budapest" to develop, but of avoiding the danger by wise, courageous and farsighted action, without first asking permission in Moscow. That was the unforgivable audacity. Nor was that all. In accordance with the will of the people, they promptly began to realize far-reaching measures of economic and political reform, humanist and democratic measures. They abolished the censorship. They introduced the secret ballot in Party elections. They passed a law on the rehabilitation of the innocent victims of the Stalin and Novotný era. Revolutionary reforms in many spheres of life were being put into practice. Much of this was still only on paper, but the press often wrote of these wished-for reforms, as if they were already real facts.

"Democratic Socialism . . ." Those were the words that horrified Ulbricht, Gomulka, and apparently Kosygin and Brezhnev as well. Will not this democracy developing in Czechoslovakia become too tempting for the other Socialist countries where the people are still living under a bureaucratic dictatorship without freedom of speech, afraid of persecution for every honest word they speak? It was at this time that Poland was waging a "struggle against Zionism" which was remarkably similar to the first performance of this game earlier, in Czechoslovakia. Not long before, Ulbricht had steamrollered the intellectuals calling for—oh, far from freedom of speech—just a little more space for creative work.

It is well known that Gomulka solved the Polish crisis in 1956 through his personal authority. When Nikita Khrushchev came to put out the Polish fire, he did not even shake hands with Gomulka at the airport.

It would be very interesting, today, to compare the program Gomulka put forward then with the speeches made by Alexander Dubček. We would find much that is similar, much in common. The only difference would be that Gomulka only talked about democracy while Dubček began to put it into practice. With his "human" promises Gomulka deceived the Polish people, giving them hopes he did not intend or at least (to be fair to him) was not allowed to and could not put into effect. Regarding these promises later as "tactics used to deal with an explosive situation," the Soviet leaders were able to forgive Gomulka. They forgave him because he did not carry out the program he had promised the people; in other words, because he deceived the nation. Czechoslovakia would not have become the problem it is if Dubček had been content with words and not tried to put his promises into effect. The Soviet leaders would have found him a clever tactician, a wise politician, "their" man.

This idea can be followed still further, and indeed it must be. The Twentieth Congress of the Communist Party of the Soviet Union brought the promise of a broad democratization and humanistic development. At that time it seemed to the whole world that the Soviet Communists had the strength to settle accounts with their own shameful past whatever the cost. What has been put into effect, of the program proclaimed by the Twentieth Congress? Nothing. There are still men in the Kremlin who have had strange careers, men who have usurped the right to decide everything and for everybody, awkward little Stalins playing at rulers of the world and great figures of history. *Socialisme, c'est moi,* could be Brezhnev's neofeudal device.

Things did not work out his way in Czechoslovakia. He was unaware of real conditions in the country, and, measuring all nations by his own, he failed to understand that the Czechoslovak people are of a different quality—not better or worse, but different—from the Russians. Those who imagined themselves great strategists, the great men of eternity, have often fallen prey to such illusory naïveté in the past. Brezhnev and his strategic advisers appear to have thought that in Czechoslovakia:

The people would rush rejoicing into the streets to welcome the tanks of their friends and liberators.

The desperate remnants of the counterrevolutionary bands would make an armed stand, thus providing supplementary, and undeniable, proof of their existence and the danger they represented.

State security forces would arrest all the leading counterrevolutionaries.

The workers' militia, so recently praised at thousands of meetings in factories, villages and towns in the Soviet Union, would come out into the streets to range themselves beside the tanks to defend their revolutionary achievements.

The workers of all the large factories would greet their liberators with enthusiastic ovations.

In the "old" National Assembly a pro-Soviet majority would promptly emerge.

The government would split and the conservatives (though without Novotný) would have the absolute majority.

The conservatives in the Central Committee of the Party would get rid of Dubček and his supporters and thus reestablish the "leading role of the Party."

Their calculations were bound to fail if only because the majority, a majority that had never been so complete and absolute, the majority of both Communists and non-Communists took their stand behind the program of the Communist Party, behind the Dubček leadership.

The Communist Party of Czechoslovakia is a legal party, with a legally elected leadership; these leaders may not have been absolutely unanimous before, but the brutal intervention of the Soviet Union in Czechoslovak internal affairs has united them now as never before. The Soviet leaders could do nothing. They had to look on while their "favorites" kept silence and even, as the real situation in the country became clear, made statements to the press and the radio stressing their support for Dubček and the other interned leaders. Except for Indra, who seemed to have fallen "sick" in Moscow out of sheer fright, and Šalgovič, not one potential ally of the Soviet forces but has publicly refuted the accusation of collaboration leveled by public opinion and sworn solemnly that they have done nothing against the true interests of the people, and that they are behind Dubček and his policy. The officers of the secret police who have been suspected and accused of willingness to collaborate have one by one declared that they are not prepared to serve the occupation authorities and that they will take orders only from their legal superiors. This is a unique and interesting psychological phenomenon. Men whom the nation had discarded and pilloried in a most disagreeable manner were asking to be trusted. In some cases the change was amazing. They behaved extremely well when people expected nothing from them. Even Novotný, the favorite Soviet supporter in Czechoslovakia for many years, although he did not condemn the occupation openly, declared that he was not prepared to collaborate in any way, and that he was retiring from public life.

Thus the Soviet guardians of Communist internationalism had

no recourse but to occupy the Party offices, lure the delegates to the Party Congress into a trap in order to intern them and try to prevent the Congress from meeting. They were not successful in this either, for the radio was on the spot, warning delegates of the trap and telling them where they should actually report.

The situation that developed was exceptionally trying and embarrassing for the Soviet Union. If they want to realize their plans in Czechoslovakia in the future, they will have first and foremost to liquidate the Communist Party, which, of course, they really came to protect from the danger of counterrevolution. On the third day of occupation, the radio was constantly announcing from various places that thousands of young people were joining the Party—students, farmers and workers. Factory branches of the Party held stormy but unanimous meetings that sent messages of solidarity, confidence and absolute loyalty to Dubček, wherever he might be. They were determined to stress the absolute legality of his position. The whole Czech and Slovak working class felt that way without exception. And does not Marx teach us that this is the class that is the guarantee, vehicle and realizer of the ideas of Socialist progress and revolution?

The Vltava broadcasting station would blather that the unarmed youngsters holding demonstrations before tanks' guns that were trained upon them were a proof of counterrevolution. Lie as they will, they cannot make black white. All right, let us assume that these few thousand youngsters are against Socialism, which is by no means sure, though theoretically possible—after all, it would perhaps be possible to find a few tens of thousands of fanatical opponents of Socialism in Czechoslovakia. Then where are the faithful supporters? Where is the mailed fist of the working class, the workers' militia? Why did they not come out into the streets, protected by the tanks, and sweep these shouting hippies away? In February, 1948, they had shown themselves able to deal with much stronger demonstrations of resistance to the will of the people. Where are your faithful supporters, dear Soviet protectors and class brothers? What has happened to them in Czechoslovakia, the most loyal base of Socialism? Have all the old Communists died out? Aren't there any left? One million eight hundred thousand Party members gone with the wind? Has counterrevolution liquidated them one and all, and replaced them with agents of the imperialists? Where are they? Did they all turn into revisionist counterrevolutionaries during the night of the fifth and sixth of January?

The goose with the strange un-Slovak accent, cackling on the Vltava station, forced to close down for two days for lack of material to broadcast, will give us the correct answer to this question. Loyal Communists are afraid of counterrevolutionary terror. This is something new in the Communist movement. One million eight hundred thousand loyal Communists have let themselves be terrorized by a couple of thousand yelling hippies. The Communists are afraid of the terrorists—when they have the fraternal aid of several thousand tanks and six hundred thousand soldiers armed to the teeth!

It is essential to find evidence. Where? At last someone had a bright idea. Arms! Arms dumps are the proof that the revanchists were planning a putsch—thirty American automatics are found under a bridge in Western Bohemia. Oh, what a terrible, mortal danger has been revealed!

That might seem terrible in the Soviet Union, where people cannot read Latin script. In Czechoslovakia we can read both Latin and Azbuka characters, and it is not difficult to make out the faded Azbuka on the wrappings, and to decipher the World War II date on the American guns. Gunmakers have the unfortunate habit of dating their products.

True, thirty old automatics is not striking proof of preparation for a putsch. More must be found. On the third day of the occupation, the free, legal radio issued a call to the workers' militia not to give up their arms. "The occupation forces intend to use your weapons as proof of an armed counterrevolutionary putsch!" And so they did, exhibiting in the Old Town Square the weapons found in counterrevolutionary arms dumps. You poor old rifles, little did you think when you were carried to Wenceslas Square in February, 1948, that a jealous fate had this in store for you!

This was all rather ridiculous and could convince no one, not even those who thought it up. A certain SS man, Naujocks, was much more convincing when in 1939 he staged an "attack on the Gleiwitz transmitter" by the Polish Army.

There is something else that is far more important. The rulers in the Kremlin were forced to sit around the conference table with those leaders of the Czechoslovak people whom they had arrested, kidnapped, carried off to an unknown destination and probably intended to get rid of. They were forced to negotiate, with the big stick, it is true, but nevertheless to negotiate with men the Soviet press was already calling revisionist traitors. They were forced to hand back to the members of the government whom they had deposed and imprisoned the status of partners in negotiation; Dubček, Černík, Smrkovský were once more fit for polite society, at least to the extent that they were brought from their place of internment and dumped down at the conference table.

These brave men did not achieve very much. What can be achieved by the government of a small country, ravished and occupied? Can they get the occupiers to retire? The Soviet leaders had expected things to turn out differently, it is true; they hoped for a compromise that would discredit Dubček, Svoboda, Černík and Smrkovský in the eyes of the people, putting them in the role of Hácha collaborators, of quislings. If they did not accept the terms dictated to them, they would never get back alive; if they did accept, they would lose the confidence of the people.

The Russian leaders did not consider the attitude of the Czechoslovak people to the Moscow negotiations; in spite of the oppressive terms dictated, the people were going to be immeasurably grateful to President Svoboda for refusing to negotiate without the interned leaders, for saving their lives. The people of Czechoslovakia bowed before the fact of the occupation, more concerned for the moment over the fate of those brave men whose lives were in danger, once they had been taken prisoner, for wanting to carry out the will of the people, risking their lives in the service of the people. Let them bring back what they could from Moscow, as long as they came back themselves, unharmed and indomitable; the rest would be taken care of by that other ally, the eternal military genius, the generalissimo of the defenseless, the good old Josef Schweik.

I want to be a prophet. Once the Soviet leaders have failed to get rid of Dubček and the others, and failed to discredit them, Soviet propagandists will find a new interpretation of their internment: they will start calling it a "safety measure" to protect them from counterrevolution. I uttered this prophecy at supper in the Budmerice Manor on August 24, and some of those present will certainly bear witness that those were my very words.

We spent the fourth night in yet another place, not any safer than the others. They are not going to start making arrests, but logic is not the only counselor. I convinced myself I was only doing it for Hannah's sake, for her to get a good night's rest, but the fears I suppressed in my own mind were too strong. Suppose they did start? Siberia is not a tempting prospect. It was not the wisest thing to do, to risk getting into trouble simply to keep up appearances, when whatever logic could say, that trouble might turn up.

Hannah fell asleep at once, tired out by the strain, but I could not drop off. It was usually the other way around, but things no longer went the usual way.

I did not fall asleep, did not want to and could not; I had too much work to do, the hardest work—to take myself in hand. I had to get my own mind straight, to admit the truth to myself after years of putting it off—when was the time if not now?

I had to balance up the ledger of my life. I had always been in the thick of things, all my life. Had I been wrong? Had the life I led, often risky and difficult, been a waste of time?

And again: am I perhaps a renegade, deviationist, Trotskyite, a wavering Communist intellectual, because I have finally found the strength to see and explain things by the light of my own reason, and not, as ordered to, the "disciplined" view?

If my reasoning takes me so far, will I have the strength of mind to admit that it was all a mistake, and therefore my whole life so far has been one long mistake?

I do not know. I cannot say. I have not yet got that far. . . .

No, I do not think it is because I have succumbed to the suggestive atmosphere in the country since January. More than once, when things still seemed to be all right, I had my doubts and reservations about the future of our democratization campaign, whether it could last and remain harmonious. It all seemed too good to be true. Our revolution for human dignity seemed very unattainable in a world that is getting more and more cynical and brutal. The world won't let us get away with it, I told myself and others, over and over again.

The Slánsky trial in 1952, and the wave of anti-Semitism connected with it, made no sense, whatever way you looked at it. What was the point of it? At that time there were not even twelve thousand Jews in the whole of Czechoslovakia; for the most part they were doctors, engineers and not political figures; they were professional men who could not easily be replaced. The fuss about Zionist public enemy number one was a piece of nonsense, all the more so since, except for the short episode of the Jewish doctors in the Soviet Union, there was no real response to it anywhere else, in spite of coordinated propaganda.

The Slánsky trial was the fourth in a series of trials in different Socialist countries, all aimed at conspiratorial centers. It was preceded by the trial of Kochi Djodj, the second most important man in the Albanian Party, accused of being a Tito spy in Albania; that of Trajcho Kostov, the second most important man in the Bulgarian Party; and that of Ladislav Rajk, the second most important man in the Hungarian Party. Those accused along with Slánsky were also mostly the second most important men in various important government departments— foreign trade, home trade, planning, finance, defense . . . but the magic figure two did not make any sense either.

And anyway, the accusations against them did not make any sense at all.

Nor was the behavior of the accused normal. Why? Had they been tortured? Exhausted? Convinced of their crimes? Hypnotized? Was some "truth drug" or other administered in their food? None of those with whom I spoke later about these questions could give me a satisfactory reply. Each reply in itself was logical, but taken together they made no sense and gave no explanation.

There were other strange things, too. Slánsky must have guessed what fate had in store for him for some time before it happened; if not at the time of the trials in Tirana and Sofia, then at least when Gomulka was imprisoned and when "contacts pointing to Czechoslovakia" were mentioned in the Rajk trial. He could not have left the country; none of them would have done that. When Clementis was warned, in New York, he answered *"Merde!"* And yet he could not have failed to realize the fatal noose was drawing tighter.

In two of the Socialist countries there were no such trials. In Romania, Georghe Gheorghiu-Dej, the hero of resistance inside the country, ousted from the political leadership the Moscow clique that was preparing the same fate for him. In the GDR, arrests had started shortly before the death of Stalin, and after that no trial was staged.

The explanation could have been Stalin. Stalin wanted it that way, Stalin gave the order . . . but there exists in Prague a document that has been preserved with Stalin's signature on it, pointing out to Gottwald the limits beyond which the Soviet advisers to the security forces cannot go, and advising him to see that this is kept to. Nor is the argument that it was all because of the Soviet experts any real explanation. The first arrests in Slovakia, when Husák, Novomeský, Holdoš, Rašla and Okályi were imprisoned, date from the time when there were as yet no Soviet experts in the country.

It is well known that Gottwald resisted pressure to have Slánsky and his fellow accused arrested; he did not want it to happen, and he held out as long as he could. We do not know who wore him down in the end and persuaded him to hand his friends over to the executioner. But if there were other forces at work, why did Gottwald not turn to Stalin for advice and aid, if the document we have is genuine?

There is not likely to be an answer to that question. The secret police—and that is another new element—burned or pulped all the documents.

The Slánsky trial itself does not offer any explanation. A long

time ago I called it "brain mold." There was neither explanation
nor justification for it. The witch-hunting mood it aroused could
not have been the sole purpose, either, and the terror let loose
in Czechoslovakia was not necessary; the country was not suffering from any economic, political or international crisis. On the
contrary, the terror and the trial brought a crisis into being. And
who was interested in creating a crisis?

Was it just an ordinary struggle for power? Who benefited
from Slánsky's fall? Not Gottwald, for the trial marked the end
of his prestige and his power. Kopecký? His position in the
Party was the same after the trial as before. Zápotocký? The
idea can only be rejected with indignation. Čepička, the Minister
of Defense? He would certainly have been capable of a plan like
that, but three years later he was out of political life himself.
Novotný did not profit from it either, for he did not come to the
limelight at all until the wave of purges put him there; he cannot
be said to have had any direct connection with the trials, since
he was not yet one of the men "in the know." Later on people
would try to blame him wrongly; his "share of the blame" does
not fit the historical facts. Novotný can only be accused of
responsibility for those excrescences that took place after his
election as First Secretary of the Party.

There remains only one explanation, and that is no explanation: the revolution devours its own children.

The Slánsky trial thus could be regarded as an arbitrary,
senseless crime. But it was not; there was a point to it, though
it cannot be seen from the trial itself, and for the explanation we
have to look elsewhere, not in the Prague or Moscow Party
secretariat but in Slovakia, small and unimportant though it may
seem. There we can find the answer to this confused problem.

Most of what has been said, although referring to Czechoslovakia, actually concerns Prague and political conditions in
Bohemia and Moravia. In Slovakia things developed more or
less differently. Thanks to the comic-opera character of the
clerico-Fascist Slovak State, the Slovak Communist Party enjoyed more favorable conditions for underground work. To be
arrested did not mean physical extinction. Mach put men in

prison and Mach let them out again. The commander of the Hlinka Guard—the Slovak counterpart to Himmler—was a jovial fellow, fond of good living, and an unstable character. It is not known how far he disbelieved his own words, or whether his meetings with well-known Communist intellectuals in the Metropole Café gave him a moral alibi, or whether he simply wanted to keep an eye on them. The fact is that they did meet and that he knew more than he gave out. He certainly must have known of the long Communist preparations for an armed rising, if only because he was told of them by the German Abwehr. In the end it was this "must have known" that saved his neck in the trial of the leaders of the clerico-Fascist government. The Communists who led the Rising gave evidence in his favor.

As was natural, Slovakia was run by men who had served in the Rising, after the liberation. Some of the outstanding *émigrés,* like Clementis, had their accepted place in the central government in exile. Positions in the regional bodies in Slovakia were divided between them by the Communist and "democratic" Rising leaders.

In the 1946 elections the Communist Party of Czechoslovakia won a clear and fairly convincing victory in Bohemia and Moravia. The 43½ percent in competition with three strong parties was more than had been expected. The Slovak Communist Party, with only one serious opponent in the Democratic Party, lost the elections, gaining only about 32 percent of the votes. That is not little, of course, but the Democrats had the rest and thus had an overwhelming majority. This defeat complicated the general position of the Communists in the National Assembly, where the Czech bourgeois parties promptly joined forces with the Slovak Democrats. The Communists had to rely on the support of the Social Democrats to secure their small and not very stable majority.

In the February, 1948, crisis, Slovakia played a passive, waiting role. That the Communists took power was not as consistent with the wishes of the people in Slovakia as it was in the rest of the country. If it were not for the fact that there was no independent Slovak policy, the term "Communist putsch" could be used here. The Communists simply drove the Democrats from their political positions by armed force. They did not have to fear any opposition. The Democratic Party never had been an organized movement with a definite program; their banner united everything that was in opposition to the Communists, from former Fascists to oversensitive supporters of a Czechoslovak democracy. In spite of their election success, the Democrats were never a serious political force, but fell apart at the first pressure from without; there was no one to defend them and no one to miss them when they were gone.

Even before the February crisis, however, the Communist Party of Slovakia was basically divided into two wings, though this was less pronounced among the membership than among the leaders. There was Viliam Široký, then the popular leader of the Party, who represented the "working-class" element in the leadership; and there was Gustáv Husák, the lawyer and intellectual, with his group of intellectuals. They had different aptitudes. While Široký sat in prison with Ďuriš, Husák and his friends prepared the Rising. Their views—I knew both of them —also differed. Husák stood for the hard line, after the Communists had come to power, while Široký appeared to be more tolerant, more patient and indulgent. It is true that at the time Široký was too busy with his work as Vice-Premier in Prague; his loyal shadow in the leadership of the Party was the faithful but inefficient general secretary, Štefan Baštovanský. Neither of the two sides took Bacílek seriously, and he occupied a subordinate position in the Executive Committee, with no power. The man of the future who made strides in his career at Široký's side was Ernest Sýkora, the young leader of the Union of Slovak Youth.

Husák had succeeded in getting the political-administrative power in his hands; his position in the Executive Committee of the Party was strong, and he had several of his own men there. He was chairman of the Regional Commissioners, the regional government of Slovakia, to which he had appointed mainly his own supporters among the intellectuals. People called it the "doctors' cabinet." Wavering between the two groups was Edo Friš, chief editor of the Party paper and a man whose past linked

him with the intellectual group, but whose years in exile with
Gottwald and Široký had made him one of their men. The Chairman of the Slovak National Council at the time was Karol
Šmidke, a fighting Communist of the old days, a worker who
flirted with the intellectuals.

It could not be long before these two groups clashed. Široký's
position in Prague was strong, but so was that of his chief
antagonist, Vladimír Clementis, Foreign Minister and member
of the Executive Committee of the Communist Party of Czechoslovakia.

In 1950 at the Ninth Congress of the Slovak Communist
Party, Široký won the day and drove his enemies from all the
decisive political positions they had held: Husák, Clementis,
Novomeský, Holdoš, Okályi, Šmidke. The justification for this
was inspired by Gottwald and confirmed at the Congress by
Rudolf Slánsky—accusations of bourgeois nationalist deviation,
placing nationalist interests above those of the working class.
This was the end of the "doctors' cabinet," efficient, active and
respected. Široký's group now ruled both the Party and the
national representative bodies. Among the Regional Commissioners, however, the intellectuals were still leading, though, with
the exception of Ondrej Pavlík, they were intellectuals who stood
behind Široký: Ján Púll, Šultész, the Social Democrat, Ernest
Sýkora, Julius Bránik, Jozef Viktory.

In the background, laughing, while all this was going on, was
Bacílek; his position was strengthened by the conflict between
the two groups without his having to take any open steps. It
would not be long, after the short episode as Minister of Security,
before he would be ruling the whole of Slovakia with his
"workers' cohorts." After Široký was moved to Prague, where
he was isolated from Slovak political life, and Štefan Baštovanský
was thrown out of his position as general secretary of the Party
and driven to suicide, Bacílek became First Secretary of the
Communist Party of Slovakia. He called to his aid the "Žilina
leaders": Pavol David, that brutal, criminal character who hated
anyone with any education, and Rudolf Strechaj, a man of iron
and a ruthless careerist.

One morning Ján Púll, a secretary of the Executive Committee, was stopped at the entrance to the Party offices by the security man on duty and told that he was not to be allowed to enter the building. "What do you think you're doing?" he retorted angrily, and when told that orders had been given . . . he went away with his head sunk between his shoulders, no longer secretary of the Party, and not even bothering to ask whose orders they were . . . to face a night of fear. Miloš Gosiorovský, secretary for ideological questions, had already been turned away in the same manner. Koloman Moškovič, a Jew and in charge of the organizational department, and Valášek, the man in charge of security, had both been dismissed as part of the campaign against Zionism.

For some time, until Bacílek returned from Prague, the central secretariat was ruled unofficially but nonetheless despotically by Pavol David, who had spent many years in the USSR and returned to Czechoslovakia after the liberation in 1945 with the rank of colonel of the NKVD (People's Commissariat of Home Affairs). Široký was going to hold out for a long time yet, as a leading statesman in Prague, but he had lost his backing, he had lost Slovakia. And the time came when the all-powerful Novotný in the Prague Executive Committee forbade Široký to appear publicly in Slovakia.

The hard line men had control of Slovak politics. The purges, trials, terror and anti-Semitism in Bohemia and Moravia seemed to make no sense, but in Slovakia things were clearer. David, primitive and brutal, purged the Party thoroughly of its intellectuals; by degrees the leading positions in the Party and in public administration were cleared of men with university degrees, and even a matriculation certificate was considered a drawback, for by the vulgar interpretation of the class struggle, workers could not acquire an education in the old bourgeois republic. All over the country "worker managers" were put in charge of big industrial enterprises, and later this usage spread; but in Bohemia and Moravia these men had at their disposal highly qualified engineers who dealt with the technical aspects of production, while the "worker manager" saw to the political side. In Slovakia all the decisive powers were in the hands of unqualified dilettantes, and to have no more than five years' elementary-school education became a virtue, one of the grounds for a successful career.

Although this purge had begun with the removal of "bourgeois nationalists" from key Party and public positions, and although Široký had dispersed the "doctors' cabinet," the tendency to get rid of the intellectuals was not yet obvious. Široký had his own set of intellectuals whom he placed in the positions vacated by Husák and his lawyers. Soon after Pavol David took over the reins, these men—Púll, Bránik and others—left, too, but for Prague, where they became Vice-Ministers.

The last intellectual in the Party Executive Committee, Ondrej Pavlík, left it in 1957, when Bacílek's gang expelled him. I learned it from Bacílek himself; he invited the writers' Party branch and informed us in a most effective manner: "Well, comrades, Ondrej Pavlík was a former member of the Hlinka Popular Party, but not in the way Comrade Strechaj or Comrade Michalička was." Then he pointed to the chairman of the Regional Commissioners on his right and the ideological secretary of the Executive Committee of the Communist Party on his left.

And that was how we came to know that there was more than one way of being a member of the clerico-Fascist party. True, you could never tell with Bacílek whether he was being naïve or funny in his own peculiar way.

One day I was in Prešov, a place I visited fairly often, and in the restaurant an enormous fellow came and sat at my table. "You don't remember me, do you?" he asked after a while. I recognized his voice; I had first known him when he always had a miner's safety helmet on his head, and then years before they had made him managing director of a big ore mine. Later I heard he'd been in prison.

"What are you doing here? Have they let you out?"

"Sure, ages ago."

"Working in the mines?"

"Sure. I'm the manager of a big opencut mine in North Bohemia. I expect you know I was in Jáchymov before that—even as a convict I was running a mine for them."

"Why don't you come back to Slovakia?"

"Don't talk to me about Slovakia. I'm all right now, nothing to complain of, and no need to be afraid they'll have me in jail again. I'll tell you what the difference between the Czechs and the Slovaks is: when I was in somebody's way in Drnava, because they wanted to give the job to that fool who managed to ruin the mine for them in a couple of years, they had to get rid of me. So they accused me of sabotage, sentenced me and sent me to jail. All right, they may want to get rid of you in Bohemia, too, if you're standing in their way. Maybe a local secretary wants some pal of his to get your job. What's he do? Calls you up and says: 'Look here, you've been convicted of sabotage; this job's too important to have you in charge, you'll have to go.' Then he gives you the best reference you've ever dreamed of. A reference that'll get you the job of manager somewhere else. They know better than to throw their engineers on the rubbish heap. Of course they weed out the people they don't want, but they don't kill you off."

Over a period of years I spent a lot of time covering the great new plant construction drive. I got to know managers and directors, building engineers and industrial engineers. When I got to know them better, I would ask any one of them: "When did they put you in jail, and for how long?"

Gradually, as I pieced my experience together, the chaotic picture began to settle. In all the purges, trials and conditions of terror, whether wrapped up in the camouflage of anti-Semitic propaganda in Bohemia and Moravia, or that of bourgeois nationalism in Slovakia, there was one primary goal aimed at: the utter destruction of the Communist intelligentsia, making it impossible for the intellectuals to have political influence at all. It was the second such thorough attempt at destruction; the first had been made by—Hitler.

You may ask—what about you? Why did nothing ever happen to you? I do not know what to say; I do not know why nothing happened to me in spite of the tense relationship between the Party leadership and me. There may have been one thing that helped—I had never taken my college entrance exams . . . that meant, or could have meant, for I do not really know, a few plus points in the assessment of my desirability.

If it were not for the personal tragedies involved, the history of Slovakia after February would read like a very funny satire about an imaginary country in an operetta. The new men in power were barely capable of reading the empty phrases their third-rate pen-pushers composed for them. I called Pavol David "Comrade Vitman," because, whenever he reached the concluding lines of his speech with the inevitable greetings to other Socialist countries, I waited for his "Long live the Vitman Democratic Republic." The Chairman of the Slovak National Council was an elderly comrade who on his election began reading his speech: "Comrades, the Chairman wishes to retort . . ."

After this man's death his place at the head of the Slovak regional assembly was taken by an incurable poacher of long standing, who was sharply criticized by this august body for trout fishing in the Orava during the closed season. The discussion that followed lasted two days: had leading officials, or had they not, the right to ignore the game and fishing laws of the country?

They were all great guys with a gun. Game shooting made them feel even more privileged, as they aped the "aristocratic" life of a defeated class, unaware that *quod licet Jovi, non licet bovi*. They would have been infinitely ridiculous in their belief that they were permanent and irreplaceable, if they had not been so dangerous. David was a terrifying figure; he was said to be unable to go to sleep at night unless he had sent at least one man to prison every day.

Under their rule Slovakia experienced sudden vast expansion and modernization of her industry, with more than her parity share of the state budget for building investments. Permanent values were created that remained and will remain. Unfortunately it was these men who had the spending of vast sums in their hands, and the result is that unprofitable, inefficient, out-of-date industries have been established for which Slovakia has neither the natural resources nor future markets. To put up in Slovakia an enormous nickel works to deal with Albanian ore which is poor in that metal is a luxury that not even a wealthy country could afford for long. The arbitrariness of these officials' "political" decisions led to violent changes in the structure of Slovak industry that did not correspond to the social needs of the country. The great textile factory on the Orava had not been finished before its purpose was changed—it was to be a non-ferrous metallurgical works instead. Of course they were not making these decisions entirely on their own, and the final approval had to come from Prague, from the government itself, and even higher, from the Executive Committee of the Party.

In 1950 the Ninth Party Congress changed the basic directives for the Five-Year Plan which was just about to get under way. Czechoslovakian industry was now to be based on heavy industry, steel. For years we tried to prove our industrial progress by quoting the amount of steel produced per head. All over the world the chief emphasis had long been placed on chemical industries with their revolutionary new opportunities in the sphere of materials. Scientists had invented new synthetics that were no mere imitations of natural materials but possessed qualities that far surpassed those produced by nature, and indeed in some cases the man-made substances possessed qualities unknown to nature. At this moment the experienced industrial country, Czechoslovakia, boasted not of the quality, but the quantity of steel she was producing. When I read this I used to recall the words of a former (alas!) leading figure in the engineering industry of Slovakia: steel means nothing; in the form of steel bars a kilogram may cost a few crowns, and in the form of watch springs it may be worth many million crowns. Both are steel.

This mania for quantity brought Czechoslovakia to an all-time low in every branch of her industry. We are no longer capable of holding our own, for quality, in competition for world markets. On the whole the civilized world does not need our industrial goods. Everything we can deliver other countries can deliver, too, of better quality, cheaper, and faster. This preferential treatment given to heavy industry was not a trend limited to Czechoslovakia. We had fairly good conditions for steel production, and sufficient cokeable coal, which is one essential. The steel and engineering tradition could have led Czechoslovakia to the same conservative attitude as England with its industrial tradition, but the emphasis laid on heavy industry was characteristic of the political economy of all the Socialist countries. Vast metallurgical works grew up in Hungary, Romania and Bulgaria, in countries where there was absolutely no reason to suppose they could prosper. In those countries, though, this development slowed down in time, and finally came to a standstill, though late. With certain changes Czechoslovakia has carried on with this policy until the present day.

Czechoslovak industry and the country's whole economy are typical victims of a "soft market." To a certain degree our exports had their guaranteed market. The West did not want to buy from us? There was the vast Eastern market open to us, with the Soviet Union, China, and all the East European Socialist countries. Soon there were also the "underdeveloped" countries of Africa, Asia and part of South America. The first time this problem struck me was during a visit to China. They took me to look at a tractor station in a rice-growing cooperative, where they had twenty tractors made in Brno. The young Chinese mechanics polished and oiled them and loved them. In China a tractor wasn't just a machine—it was a little god! Yet in the rice-growing region to which they had been sent, they were of very little use in the form in which we had sold them. Where the rice fields are under water, there is only a very short time of the year when tractors can be effectively used to plow the ground when it has dried out.

The atomization of Czechoslovak industry, producing industrial goods in 70 percent of the world's categories, made it highly attractive to the industrially underdeveloped Socialist countries. In small quantities we could put on the market goods which they had not the hard currency to buy elsewhere. Tractors? In countries where they had never seen a tractor before, the outdated Czechoslovak type of tractor was a great help. Give us as many as you can!

In such favorable conditions, who would bother about improving the design of a new series of tractors? Our clients were willing to buy series that even our benevolent quality control had rejected. Not even the new phenomenon of Western penetration into the Socialist market sufficed to alarm our politicians and economists to the danger. That's nothing, that can't affect our market.

In 1960 I spent a few days in Moscow, where Italian and Hungarian shoes had appeared in the shops for the first time. A year earlier the people of Moscow would stand in long lines when it was rumored that there would be Czechoslovak shoes for sale. This time I walked about the streets, met friends and talked to strangers, and both friends and strangers asked me: "Why do you make such ugly shoes, of such poor quality?" There was a mood of protest against Czechoslovak shoes in the streets of Moscow. It was absurd, especially since it was largely because of the import of tens of millions of pairs of Czechoslovak shoes every year that the people were at least shod. Absurd perhaps, from that point of view; but not absurd from the Czechoslovak point of view. It was then that the Czechoslovak footwear industry was boasting of having reduced the number of types of shoe produced to eighty. This kind of standardization was typical of the whole of our industry at that time, confusing "economic effectiveness" with "large series." This was another consequence of the soft market.

In this economic system, the growing young industries of Slovakia had their special place. One of the characteristic features of the distribution of industrial investment in Slovakia was the tendency to place industry where there was a labor supply. In its way this was a charitable enterprise. Was there a poverty-stricken corner in Slovakia, a poor agricultural spot? Industry would bring work, and with it a higher standard of living, a better and more civilized way of life, furthering Socialist progress, training new working-class cadres. The factories would become bastions of Socialism in backward areas with their religious prejudices.

This might have been a wise move, if attention had also been paid to the economic side; unfortunately, this was not the rule. How could it be, when such "political decisions" came from the minds of men who could make such incredible statements as:

"We are not going to insist on increased production of nylon stockings and underwear, comrades. As you know, they are very durable and can be worn for a long time, and that means the demand falls and there might be a falling-off in the number of girls needed in the stocking factories. That is not the way Socialist industry can develop."

The author of this profound economic truth was Karol Bacílek. Is it any wonder that in the course of time every citizen of the Republic understood his constitutional right to work as being the right to do the job he happened to be doing at that moment? This meant the anomaly of creating artificial employment, in spite of a permanent overall shortage of labor, and still worse, it meant that Czechoslovak industry fell behind the rest of the world in modernization.

There were sometimes serious shortcomings in the investment plans themselves, which adversely affected the results of the efforts put into them by both our nations. In 1954, the tenth anniversary of the Slovak National Rising was solemnly celebrated in Banská Bystrica. It was remarkable for the fact that on the platform for prominent heroes and guests, people who had actually taken part in the Rising were decidedly in the minority; most of the military and partisan leaders celebrated the anniversary in jail. The chief speaker was Karol Bacílek, and after the speeches were over, he was approached by a delegation of district and municipal officials who asked him to approve a certain change in the plans for the big new cement plant to be built outside the town. In a detailed memorandum experts had proved that the plans did not take into account the direction of the wind; if the plant was to stand on the spot proposed, Banská Bystrica, the jewel of all the Slovak towns, of which the proverb says, "Live in Bystrica on earth and in heaven afterwards," this lovely town would be showered with ash and heavy cement dust, particularly since the heating equipment was planned for poor quality fuel. The delegation put forward an alternative plan, because all agreed that a cement plant was needed; it should stand on the other side of the town, to leeward, in a valley where conditions for obtaining the raw materials were ideal: excellent quality limestone. The local draftsmen promised to do all the necessary work on their own time, without payment, so that there would be no increase in costs.

Bacílek did not even hear them out.

"What?" he shouted angrily. "I won't have my industrialization program ruined by any narrow-minded bourgeois in Bystrica!"

That was that. Period. All decided. The delegation left him, depressed, and he felt he was a man of action, solving problems on the spot, reacting with lightning political decision.

The cement plant was built. In the years since then it has covered the town with a blanket of heavy white dust. After you have been there for a few hours, if you run your hand over your face, it may leave a bloody scratch as you rub the sharp particles of the ash into your skin.

The cement plant was built on the spot originally decreed, of course, as in so many other cases, without the necessary geological research, on a small limestone deposit that was soon exhausted. Now there is an overhead transport system, several miles long, to bring in the stone. It is quarried in the very spot where the experts and officials, well acquainted with local conditions, had wanted the cement plant to stand, at the foot of a hill of first-class limestone. Karol Bacílek has lived to see the time he perhaps did not wish to see, a time when high officials relegated to the background need no longer find themselves either in a hospital bed with a heart attack, or in jail. He has retired on a pension, and walks about Bratislava waxing indignant over the way we are making a mess of Socialism; he recalls the days when he was making lightning decisions, sharp, penetrating, and genius-like, on every aspect of the life of the state. Everything worked properly then, nothing ever went wrong, for he and his followers would never have allowed those damn intellectuals to stick their noses in everywhere, interfering in political affairs, the intellectuals who are now getting the upper hand and want to bury our wonderful Socialism.

I have one very pleasant memory of his years in office. In

1958 I consented for three months to stand in for the secretary of the Union of Slovak Writers. At that time Bacílek was very actively interested in cultural questions and would invite the Communist members of the cultural unions to discussions in which he confused monologue with dialogue and often talked himself without a break for two or even three hours.

One day he sent for me, sat down in an armchair and, instead of starting away back in the old times with his not uninteresting memories, jumped right *in medias res*.

"What do you writers think about the cosmopolitanism in Slovak music?"

I stiffened, and my mind feverishly tried to see the connection.

Cosmopolitanism in Slovak music . . . which of the composers or conductors or players was a Jew? I could not think of anyone. Cosmopolitanism . . . you couldn't say that of Suchoň, or of Cikker, or of Moyzes . . . nor the young composers.

I waited to see what was going to come next.

"Well," he went on, after enjoying my discomfiture, "we have nothing against the young people, that is the Party has nothing against their enjoying themselves in their own way, if they like this hopping about they call dancing, if they prefer jazz to our beautiful folk songs, all right. But things are going too far. Even jazz ought to have a national form, worthy of the nation. All these cosmopolitan texts in foreign tongues, this I luvyoujevoos-emichliebedich stuff has got to stop. We are going to propose to the Executive Committee that the radio and television programs should forbid such cosmopolitan nonsense that has nothing to do with our Socialist patriotism. What do you say to that?"

What did I say to that? I agreed. It was enormously important for the healthy development of our young people. It would be another nail in the coffin of the warmongers.

He agreed with me. Yes, that was just what he had thought himself.

Bacílek was not the worst. He was more tolerant than some of them, and during his short term as Minister of Security, he was the first person to release innocent victims from jail. In 1954 he released one of the Social Democrat groups imprisoned in Slovakia, and that was at least something in view of his unpredictability. You could never tell why he did one thing and did not do another. There is no justification for the accusation that he was primarily responsible for the Slánsky trial and those that followed it. He did not become minister until after Slánsky had been arrested, when the witch-hunt was on with a vengeance, if not nearing its end, for the secret police by then were completely in the hands of Soviet experts—whom Khrushchev had shot after the shooting of Beria, by the way. Bacílek could not change anything as far as the accused were concerned, either for the better or for the worse; everything had been prepared by others before he came on the scene. He simply lent his name to it. Several years later, at one of those discussions he used to invite us to, Vladimír Mináč and I asked him outright about his share of the responsibility for the trials. He burst into tears.

"Comrades," he said in defense, "if I committed any crime, if what I did can be called a crime, then it was only my absolute and uncritical confidence in our Soviet comrades."

Even later, during the "Prague spring" of 1968, he would reveal what everybody knew but he was the first to say aloud: that the chief Soviet expert during the trials was Anastas Mikoyan. The journalists would accuse him of saying this as an alibi, of trying to distract attention from his own responsibility, but that is not necessarily true. It is quite possible that after he was deprived of power in the Party Bacílek came to see quite a few things in their true light. It would not be the first time I had seen an official, after being kicked out to spend some time in ordinary civil life, having his eyes opened to all sorts of things.

I have no cause to make him sound better than he was. I know that he was more than once willing to help, although not always, nor was his help always proportionate to the justice of the case. I managed to get him to set several innocent victims free. If it was a Slovak case, which the Slovak organs could decide alone, I always went to him about it. He cursed me for it, but when he felt like it he would help, and that was a lot, especially for people who were suffering unjustly. Except for one case I never went to Novotný.

Bacílek's greatest sin was his incredible naïveté. The day he burst into tears in front of us was one such example: he felt he ought to try to shift some of the blame, and so he told us that some of the people we were anxious to help were very ingenious rogues who deserved all they had got.

"I got a letter from a convict," he said, "complaining about the very bad treatment he was suffering, being beaten up and not given anything to eat and goodness knows what else. I wanted to see for myself what it was all about, and so I drove straight down to Bory, that's a prison near Pilsen, where he was. I got them to bring him out, and he didn't know where to look—said all he'd written was untrue, that he was only trying to draw attention to himself in order to get released on probation. What do you say to that?"

We said nothing. Our heads hanging, some of us embarrassed, some of us grinning. A pity the convict didn't confess it was all the other way around, and he was beating up his warders and not giving them enough to eat and torturing them. Bacílek would have swallowed it.

Formally he was number one Party man, but the real ruler of Slovakia, the monster, was the number two man, Pavol David. The terror he instituted in Slovakia as soon as he became secretary to the Executive Committee was so unbearable and so dangerous that we writers, who were his most hated enemies, found it necessary to defend ourselves. It was in Slovakia that the first outspoken resistance to arbitrary terror was heard. It was not that our lives were endangered; I know of no writer imprisoned for his literary work alone; Novomeský was a member of Husák's group and was convicted of political crimes, while the Czech writer Jiří Mucha was accused of espionage. It was not done to put writers in jail, and that may have been one of the reasons why David hated us so much. What we were concerned for was the opportunity to publish, our existence as writers; we wanted the right to create truthful and forceful literary works; we did not want to have police spies on our tails all the time, watching our wives' shopping baskets; and above all we wanted to put an end to the terrible ravishment and crushing of the nation.

I was one of the first to rebel. In the pages that follow I shall be describing mainly my own experience, but that does not mean I was alone in the struggle—it would not even have been possible. There were not many of us, but we stood by one another, defending each other, and not letting the worst happen to any one of us. We all suffered bad moments. If there was any way in which I differed from the rest, it was only in having strong nerves and a somewhat unusual way of fighting. Some of them dealt with things logically, but logic is no weapon against a bureaucratic dictatorship. Just as our adversaries knew how to find their victim's weakest spot, those who fought them had to use their weaknesses against them. It was no good appealing to their reason, their generosity, or their humanity. David, a man with no sense of humor, would have laughed at any such approach.

One had to go for David in a different way. He hated all writers, and Vladimír Mináč and myself in particular. He was afraid of us, afraid of our open impudence, our impertinent glances, our insolent arrogance.

At a garden party given by the Polish consul in Bratislava, he came up to our table with a pretzel he had been chewing in his hand, and offered me a bite.

"Not me," I replied, "when you've been licking it."

"My God, can't it rain?" Vladimír Mináč sighed, next to me.

"What's that?" David roared at him. "My God, did you say? You bloody hypocrites, pretending to be educated Marxists and underneath you're all God-fearing skunks."

They had to get him away from our table, he was in such a state of fury.

"My God . . ." I remembered a wonderful scene I had witnessed when he was regional secretary of the Party in Žilina and I was working there for a time on the regional paper. It was a Sunday, and for some reason he was making a speech on a plat-

form put up for the occasion close to the Catholic church. Mass
had just finished and the people were coming out—among them
his own wife! She went straight from the church door to his side
on the platform, in front of several thousand people—naturally
they enjoyed it mightily. So that was how it was at home. He
was obviously helpless to do anything about it, and that was why
any mention of God sent him raving mad.

On one occasion a ceremonial dinner was held at the Carlton
Hotel in honor of a certain visiting ambassador. For some unknown reason I was among those invited. I came a little late and
found the guests of honor already toasting one another. David
spied me and hurried up to me, fighting mad.

"Hey, you, Mňačko, we two are going to fight like hell one
of these days."

I looked him in the eye, half a head taller than he was, and
answered him with calm ridicule:

"We can't fight, Comrade David."

He couldn't understand that.

"Why not? Why shouldn't we?"

"We two can't fight, because it takes two to make a fight, and
the minute we started I'd land such a blow you wouldn't know
what'd hit you. That's not a fight, that's wiping the floor with
you."

What followed was like the last scene of Gogol's *Inspector*.
All those watching were turned to stone.

That was the only way to hold your own and keep men like
David in fear of you. The more fearless our behavior, the more
arrogant our insults, the more they feared us.

The scandals I caused were deliberate, and however strange
it sounds, every one of the long series increased those big bugs'
respect for me and those like me. At a meeting of writers and
artists called by the Executive Committee (the Party could not
expect to get results out of the writers alone), we were to condemn the anti-Party views of Vladimír Mináč contained in a
manuscript that had never been published and that none of those
present had seen. The Commissioner of the Interior, Oskár
Jeleň, a shady figure of the time who should not have been

allowed to sink into oblivion, objected to Mináč's having a higher income than a Commissioner earned. I shouted at the top of my voice: "That's a lie!" and in the dead silence that ensued I went on:

"I know what your pay is and I know what Vladimír Mináč's income is. It's high, though I don't see why it should be discussed here. If you want to discuss it, I can tell you that I live in the same house as two Commissioners, and I can give you a pretty exact idea of what they earn on the side."

Bacílek interrupted me: "Let's drop the subject; it doesn't really concern the matter in hand." In the end he tried to excuse himself. Even the Executive Committee may make a mistake, and not prepare a meeting properly, and "as you have seen, comrades, we are not without our weaknesses, too."

In full view of several members of the Executive Committee, I gave the cultural dictator of Slovakia a good beating; he was a creature full of pathological hatred whom all the unions had been trying to get removed for ten years; that was almost a reason to keep him, of course, because if they were all against him, it was clear he was doing his job well. I beat him up and smashed his face in, and three months later he was out on his neck in disgrace.

I was hauled over the coals by the supreme Party inquisition, the Party Control Committee, for constantly insulting members of the Executive Committee of the Party, members of the Slovak National Council and high public officials. After three hours of arguing, I was just going out when they told me that disciplinary measures would be taken and that I should be given a Party sentence.

"You are wrong, comrades," I laughed at them impudently. "There won't be any sentence for me, but I can tell you now who is going to be sentenced—you, all three of you, as sure as you sit there. You are infringing the rules of the Party, the principles of the Party, the moral strength of the Party . . . you are infringing everything that can be infringed."

They stared at me, pale and shocked, as though I was a ghost. Nobody had ever dared to speak to them like that before. To them! Everyone called before their august presence stood there trembling, explaining, begging, confessing . . . That was the place for humility and humiliation. Who was it that dared to stand up to them? Who could he have behind him, to make him so bold? Which of the great and powerful, greater and more powerful than they themselves? Who could be greater and more powerful than they were?

The chairman of the committee told me they would have to consider the matter again; they had not yet agreed on a decision.

"Consider it again, comrades, by all means consider it again! But this time, mind you, do it by the right standards!"

There were no disciplinary measures. Nor did I get any Party sentence.

Shock them, shock them any way you can. Pretend to be in a stronger position than they are. Break through the accepted convention of behavior, react in a way they don't expect. Self-criticism at a Party meeting? In front of you damn lot of hypocrites? No, you'll never hear that from me, never.

"You shut up, I'm keeping you and your many children," I shouted at an editor who had accused me of undisciplined behavior, in front of a Party meeting. "You may sit here twelve hours a day, but your inefficiency cries to heaven. Let's see some of your work and compare it with mine—and then you can start talking. Only make it modest!"

They proposed expelling an incorrigible skirt-chaser from the Party and firing him from the paper "for immorality." I had only to ask: "Are we going to deal with his case only, or shall I add details of all the cases known to me, for the information of this court of morals?"

The proposal did not get far. Almost everybody present voted against it.

"The nation has no respect for you, you ought to resign," I told Novotný to his face, before witnesses. The simple fact that I used the "you" and not the "thou" form was enough to put him in a rage, for he thought I was laughing at him. One day, at the Castle, hanging on to Ahmed Ben Bella, to whom he wanted to introduce me, he cried: "How do you do, *Mister* Mňačko?"

Only a short while afterward he subjected me to severe criticism at a meeting of the Central Committee, calling me "someone by the name of Mňačko." I would not stand for that, and sent him a message to say that I was as much a Party member as he was, and that since we were both equal before the Party, I referred to him in public as Comrade Novotný; that I thought the basic rules of decent politeness ought to be observed in the Party, and that as the foremost man in the Party he should be especially careful to see that they were. Vladimír Mináč and I did all we could to shock and provoke. When we felt like being scandalous, we would sing Tito songs in the café, especially the one that goes:

> *Molotova i Stalina, i Stalina,*
> *Molotova i Stalina!*

On two different occasions I beat up two secret police spies and left them lying on the ground. Mináč dealt with his "shadow" in an even more appropriate manner: he waited for him in a dark corner, spoke to him and invited him to have a drink. When he was good and truly drunk, Mináč said: "Now say what a damned spying swine you are." Then he carted him to all the bars for a week, every night, the secret policeman, like a trained monkey, hanging on his neck and weeping: "You're a wonderful guy, you're really a wonderful guy, and I'm a Judas, a damn little Judas."

In a Prague bar we "arrested" a secret police officer and took him to my apartment with his eyes blindfolded. Then we interrogated him for seven hours. He broke down and wept three times; he didn't realize that what he was doing was wrong, he thought it was his duty. When we threw him down the steps, I warned him we'd recorded it all on tapes and now we had him where we wanted.

"You want to go down in history? Don't worry, you'll be there all right, and all the dirty things you've done, not a single one will be forgotten. You rely on people forgetting, but nothing will be forgotten—for everything you've got on your conscience, there'll be a witness. I, for example, have a perfect memory," I threatened this high, powerful official. The bolder and more arrogant we got, the more gently they handled us, the humbler and more "friendly" they were. And what is even stranger, they went out of their way to come up against us, talk to us, out of a defensive need to convince us they were not as stupid as we were always making them out to be, or so evil as we thought.

In 1964, Harry Pross asked me at a press conference in Bremen how it was that nothing had ever happened to me.

"I can't say," was my answer. "Perhaps I've just been lucky, but more likely it's because I was always impudent."

That same year, when I headed the editorial office of *Kulturný Život* for a few months, we always went through the same business every Wednesday, the day we went to press. Everybody turned up in the morning, and I never forgot to forbid any drinks until the paper was on press. Instead I put four pounds of caramels on the desk to keep our strength up. Some of us went to the printers to deal with last-minute corrections, and the rest waited in the office. That day all the typists stayed on until the evening, the messenger waited, too, and we all sat in tense expectation of what the evening would bring. About six o'clock, when we ought to have been thinking of starting the presses, the phone would ring and we knew it would be the head of the "nonexistent" censor's office and that he would ask for me.

"Tell him," I shouted to my deputy, loud enough for him to hear at the other end of the line, "that I've nothing to say to him. We've been asking long enough for him to be given an intelligence test. I'm the chief editor here, and as long as I am here I'm going to decide what goes in. If he has anything to say he can say it to you."

Of course he had something to say. Six pages out. Never five and never seven. It was always six. Six pages he couldn't let past; we'd have to find something else.

"Tell him I haven't got anything else, and even if I had I wouldn't do it. If he doesn't put that green stamp on it, the paper won't come out at all."

That day the whole of the ideological department at Party headquarters was always on the job. The head of the department and the secretary for ideological questions, Bil'ak, both stayed on. They knew what was coming. In the end I got them to agree to cut three sentences.

"Two or three sentences don't matter, comrades; I'm always ready to come to terms."

I never agreed to censor a whole article, or to make cuts that would distort the author's meaning.

We did an interview with Marie Švermová, saying that Rudolf Slánsky had not murdered Jan Šverma in the Slovak mountains. The Central Committee phoned the secretary for ideological questions in Prague, Vladimír Koucký, now our ambassador to Moscow. He put his foot down. It would not be allowed through.

I was there while they talked to him.

"Tell him the paper won't come out, then. I won't let the paper go to press with an article missing."

They told him and he gave way. The interview appeared.

It was the same way week after week. We celebrated every issue with a wild drinking party. These Wednesday relaxations swallowed up twice my salary as chief editor. When they didn't know what to do about us, they surrounded us with police spies. We opened all the windows and shouted a vulgar song contemptuously into the street.

One week they were all in Prague for a meeting of the Central Committee. I was very worked up that evening; the chief censor was a law unto himself. He did not ask for six pages this time, but for one article on the front page. It was an article that could but need not have been printed. There was nothing in it the censor could object to, except that it was signed by a writer who was in disgrace at the time.

I yelled in my usual way, close to the receiver, that I had nothing else ready, and even if I had I wouldn't put it in. Something unusual happened. The censor replied quite calmly that if I hadn't and wouldn't, then he wouldn't either, and there'd be no green stamp.

I dug my heels in and so did he.

The paper did not come out.

I went up to Prague that night to be out of their way.

The paper did not come out the next day, nor the day after. On the fourth day, comrades from the ideological department caught up with me. I still refused to leave out the article, but said I didn't want to create difficulties, and if they liked I'd give up the job. They did, and I gave it up. The paper came out in a much bigger edition than usual, five days late, and people fought for it. They looked to see "what all the trouble was about," but they didn't find it. And even if they had, they would have been disappointed, because there really was nothing in the article that the censor could object to.

Two weeks before the press conference I mentioned, in Bremen, I was called to the Central Committee offices and asked to allow my name to remain on the paper as chief editor, until after the press conference, so as "not to cause an international scandal." I did not want to cause international scandals, and so when they asked me in Bremen about my job as chief editor, I replied that I was still in the job, for the time being, but that I had only taken somebody else's place for a few months, and that it would soon be over.

I still thought, then, that it wasn't right to create international scandals. Before long, though, I said to myself that if that was what they were afraid of, that was what they ought to get. When I started writing my book *The Taste of Power,* I told the managers of the publishing house where the book was to appear in Czechoslovakia, and with whom I had a contract, that I did not know whether they would be able to publish it or not, but that it meant a lot to me, and if it didn't appear in Czechoslovakia, it would have to appear abroad, in the West.

They smiled. The very idea that any writer would dare to do such a thing was absurd, although they were prepared to hear all sorts of things from me.

I said the same thing to the Party people who had to do with cultural matters. They smiled, too.

The scandal over the publication of this book by Molden, the Vienna publisher, who brought out the German-language edition, burst a few hours after I had left for Vietnam in the plane taking a government delegation there. The contract I had signed with Molden had been in Prague for weeks, lying in the offices of Dilia, the monopoly agency through which Czechoslovak writers have to arrange their contracts with foreign publishers.

I had made myself thoroughly familiar with the law, I knew how full of holes it was. The law provides that "the author of a literary work or work of art arranges contracts with foreign firms through the agency of a Socialist organization." Nobody could prove that I had tried to do anything else. I felt very much inclined to bring a case against Dilia, after I got back to Czechoslovakia, for having failed to ratify the contract. There is absolutely nothing in the wording of the law to suggest that Dilia can refrain from ratifying a contract with a foreign firm. The regulations governing which foreign countries were to be offered which literary works by Dilia were in no law, but were part of the illegal censorship set up outside the laws of the country. In practice, of course, the political advisory committee carried out a preliminary censorship of the books concerned, according to which Dilia was allowed to recommend certain books and not others, to arrange contracts for some authors and not for others. There were books that were not allowed to be published abroad at all. There were books that were allowed to be published only in Socialist countries. Strange as it may seem, there were books that were allowed to be published only in the capitalist world. And there were books that could be published anywhere in the world. From this point of view, the passage of the law which lays down the procedure for arranging contracts abroad is not as stupid and illogical as it seems.

This law is typical of the pliability and the loopholes so frequent in Czechoslovak legal formulation. The broadest interpretation is possible, and any amount of manipulation. The loopholes made it possible for the authorities to manipulate the laws as they chose, for many years, and even to attribute to them a meaning opposite to the one intended.

Now, at last, they had got something against me. Why should I have the monopoly of scandal at their expense? Now they could turn one of the scandals against me. Accusations thundered out at Party meetings, in the government, in government departments, in the artists' unions, in both the writers' unions. I was far away and defenseless. They wanted to make sure they had me in a spot. They wanted to finish me off before I got back. They knew that the accusations against me were false, and so they had to discredit me before I could answer back. Novotný insisted I be expelled from the Party. The committee of the Writers' Union was to condemn the "incorrect" procedure publicly. They had plenty of time; I had planned to stay five months in Vietnam. The Western press linked this visit with the scandal about the book, but the two things were not related. I had gone to Vietnam of my own accord, not as a punishment. It was the authorities who used my absence to try and put me in an impossible position.

When the book was published by Molden in March, 1967, the affair had already blown over. I dropped on them literally from the skies, right in the middle of the scandalous campaign against me, which reached its climax just at the time of my return.

My guess as to what direction the campaign against me would take, and what means they would employ, was fairly correct. It did not worry me too much, but I decided to cut short my visit to Vietnam. At the end of the third month, I asked Prague to let me return by the southern route, through Cambodia. But matters were so arranged that I had to travel by the northern route. They wanted to keep contol of me. I informed the embassy in Peking of my arrival, and they were waiting for me at the airport. I should have been helpless without them, for the cultural revolution was at its height. I spent several days there watching the marching Red Guards and listening to their rhythmic shouting.

I asked the embassy to send a coded cable to Moscow saying when I expected to arrive and asking for a room, as I would like to spend a few days there. On landing in Moscow, I immediately boarded the plane for Prague, on which there was a seat vacant.

I had been in Prague for three days before the telegram announcing my imminent arrival from Moscow came in, right into the middle of the discussion of my affair.

The moment I arrived I went into counterattack. "A dirty business!" I shouted loudly enough for everyone in the place to hear. "The book should have appeared in Slovakia before it came out in Vienna. I had a contract to that effect. This is an infringement of my contract! I have done nothing that was not correct. Dilia should have ratified the contract; it says so in black and white. I signed the contract with Molden after I had already signed two valid contracts for the Czech and Slovak editions. The three Party men competent to decide questions of cultural policy, Hendrych, Koucký, and Auersberg, all read the manuscript. I acted with a sense of responsibility and gave them the manuscript to read because I realized the political implications of the book."

I managed to convince the committee of the Writers' Union that I had intended to arrange the contract with Molden through Dilia, as indeed I had. If Novotný had not prohibited the publication of the book in Czechoslovakia, it would have appeared in Prague first and in Vienna later, and there would have been no scandal at all. At the committee meeting it came out that when Auersberg, head of the ideological department of the Central Committee and prime mover of the campaign against me, was reading the incriminating contract to them in my absence, he omitted the passage about Dilia. I turned the attack against him. That was nothing less than a dirty piece of work.

Auersberg denied it. So did another big bug, Hendrych, then Party man number two. He declared before the disciplinary commission that he had never set eyes on the manuscript and never had spoken to me about it. Sometime later one of the leading Czech writers asked me what line Hendrych was taking over the book. I told him Hendrych had denied ever having read it or ever having mentioned it to me.

"The swine! The cursed swine! I had supper with him one night and he talked of nothing else but how important and how interesting your book was and how it ought to come out as soon as possible." He was prepared to give me that in writing if I needed it, and was ready to swear to it in personal confrontation with Hendrych.

There followed two months of distasteful squabbling; the commission put their proposal for my punishment—a severe reprimand (the severest penalty short of expulsion)—before the Executive Committee, and Novotný returned it for "more detailed information." He insisted I should be expelled, but the commission did not want to give in to dictation. In the end he got the worst of it, because members of the Executive Committee were so tired of his obstinacy that they accused him of acting from personal spite and refusing to accept the view of the majority. So I was punished as they proposed, and Novotný got a telling-off from the Committee, probably the first he had ever been given.

The public had been following all this with unconcealed delight.

It was during this period that my skepticism and distrust of Soviet foreign policy reached its climax. My three months in Vietnam had made me think deeply; what was so peculiar about that war? American planes were constantly patrolling over Haiphong harbor, and I tried to put myself in their place. The port was full of cargo vessels, most of them Soviet ships, and it was not difficult to see from the air what was being unloaded from them. Rockets, antiaircraft guns, fighter planes. The American pilots could not help thinking with cold fright: which of those rockets has got my number on it? Which of those guns is going to get me? Yet neither before nor since has a single bomb been dropped on that harbor. The American pilots were forced to look on while those freighters disgorged death—their death, the death of American pilots. Why did they not bomb the harbor? They might damage a Soviet ship, it might lead to protests, to a freeze-up of the polite good relations between America and the Soviet Union, to a stepping-up of international tension.

I am on the side of the people of Vietnam, 100 percent; I was then and I am now, particularly since the occupation of Czechoslovakia. I have seen how they live and fight and die and work and long for things and rejoice in things. I have eaten rice with them from one bowl, slept on their matting in their huts with them. I admire the genius of this small nation which has been able to cope with all the problems and the suffering of thirty years of almost incessant warfare. Then I wrote that the clash in Vietnam was not the traditional clash between Communism and capitalism, and recent events in Czechoslovakia have borne me out. The Americans have no business in Vietnam, where nobody wants them. The Soviet soldiers have no business in Czechoslovakia, where nobody wants them.

I was not a member of the official Czechoslovak delegation, but only thankful for a seat in the official plane, into which I could get all my overweight. I paid my own expenses for this trip to Vietnam, just as I always paid my own expenses on such journeys.

I was not a member of the government delegation, but I had the opportunity to see them at work. On our way there we stopped off in Moscow, where our statesmen met Kosygin and Brezhnev. The second stop, in Peking, was an exciting affair. We were met at the airport by the Foreign Minister, Ch'en I. It was the first time I had witnessed a "cold welcome." Ch'en I gave a supper for us, but neither he nor Premier Josef Lenart made any special effort to be cordial. I have rarely enjoyed a meal less. I was in fairly close touch with the delegation all the time in Vietnam, although I went around on my own from the very first day. I listened carefully to what was said at meetings, at receptions. In the course of its development, Communist phraseology has evolved ways of expression which you have to know how to decipher. I was already master of this art, and could feel the tension behind the smiles, the profound problems beneath the phrases about eternal friendship and undying love. What were our statesmen trying to do? It seemed to me that they were bringing pressure to bear on their Vietnamese colleagues, trying to get Ho Chi Minh not to come out against discussion of the Vietnam problem at the General Assembly of the United Nations even if representatives of North Vietnam were not to be invited to take part. That was how it sounded: don't you worry, we'll take care of it.

It was unthinkable that this was an independent step in foreign policy on the part of Czechoslovakia; it sounded as though we were doing the Soviets' dirty work for them, in obvious contradiction to the official declarations of "unreserved support for the fight of the people of Vietnam against imperialist aggression."

Later, on endless exhausting trips, I saw how poorly equipped the army of Vietnam was to stand up to the terrible destructive force of the American Army. The MIG-17 planes could not fight as the equals of the American planes. The antiaircraft guns were out of date. At that time there was very little in the way of antiaircraft rockets. Soviet accusations of Chinese "sabotage" of help to Vietnam were a very threadbare excuse with no basis in fact. Later this situation changed, but at this moment the effect was just that.

The people of Vietnam were successfully standing up to the Americans with the little they had at their disposal. Maybe if the firing capacity and mobility of Vietnam's forces had been increased then, things would look different now. I could not conceal my fury, less than a year later, when I saw the enormous scrap heap of Sinai. When I was in Vietnam, the people there had none of the equipment I saw lying rusting in the Sinai Desert. With that firing capacity, they would have driven the Americans into the sea.

After what I saw in Vietnam, I could not get rid of the feeling that the Soviet Union was not playing a straight game in foreign affairs and that there was something going on between her and the United States, something that the small nations would have to suffer for.

This was the reason for the most scandalous of my scandals, my spectacular departure for Israel. I attacked Czechoslovak foreign policy, furiously and ceaselessly, but without the slightest risk that I would be misunderstood, for there was no such thing as Czechoslovak foreign policy. There could have been; Czechoslovakia could have had a foreign policy at least as distinctive as Romania's, but we would have had to have a different man than Novotný as President.

In 1960 I was invited to the regional Party conference in

Bratislava as a guest. The Central Committee delegation was headed by Rudolf Barák, then the Minister of the Interior, a dangerous demagogue and a ruthless careerist. From the platform he enunciated several extraordinary statements that, it must be admitted, earned him frenetic applause.

It must be unique in European politics for a Minister of the Interior in a Socialist state to declare: "I must tell you, comrades, that the West German Free Europe transmitter is controlled by me. I've got my people there, and whatever suits us to have Free Europe broadcast goes out on the air in a couple of hours, or in three days at the latest."

It is usual for a Minister of the Interior to issue an indignant denial when his agents are caught *in flagrante delicto* and their espionage activity is proved. For the Minister himself, of his own accord, to boast of the effectiveness of his spy service and even of the place where it is working is a remarkable piece of stupidity, assuming that his statement was true.

But this particular Minister went even further.

"I expect you know, comrades, that Comrade Novotný and I were in Moscow at that great meeting of Communists from all over the world, the conference of Communist and workers' parties. Discussion was not always easy, I can tell you. Some of the delegations from the Socialist countries were difficult to deal with.

"When we appeared and Comrade Khrushchev caught sight of us, he left the people he was talking to and came over to us, delightedly slapping us on the shoulder and hanging around our necks. . . . 'Comrades from Czechoslovakia,' he said, 'we don't have any trouble with you, do we? Know what? Let's go to the ballet this evening instead of talking business.'

"And during the intermission, in his box at the theater, Comrade Khrushchev leaned over and said, 'Don't worry, comrades; don't you be afraid of anybody. If anything should happen . . . the Germans . . . in an hour we're on your frontiers.' "

Frenetic applause. The delegates sitting at the table where I was frowned angrily. Who was this intruder who dared to sit there and not clap? During a break one of them stopped me in the corridor and said:

"What did Barák say about them being on our frontiers in an hour? The atom war will be over in an hour, won't it?"

You could believe Barák's statement that that was really what was said in Moscow. The Soviet leaders never had to bother discussing anything with Novotný, because there were no differences of opinion between them—least of all in foreign policy. And what other questions are there for two sovereign states to discuss, except those of foreign policy? That is certainly a naïve question, in view of the way the Soviet Union treats her allies. And when the other questions, those that do not concern foreign policy, are not worth talking about, then the attitude of the smaller state to the powerful one is that of a servile vassal doing in advance everything his master is going to wish next day.

That Novotný's policy was such, throughout his reign, Barák did not need to stress with such enthusiasm. It was strange. Novotný and his system ruined the Czechoslovak economy, desecrated the idea of Socialism until it attracted the nation less and less, discredited the Party and its policy and prestige, and brought the country slowly but surely to the verge of bankruptcy. The Kremlin rulers did not see in this any danger to Socialism; in the distortion of Marxism and Leninism they did not see any "revisionism." As long as Novotný was in power, he and his Kremlin masters thought everything in Czechoslovakia was fine, and could serve the other Socialist nations as an example; we were flattered at being considered their most loyal and best beloved friends and allies. Czechoslovakia was the strongest bastion of Socialism outside the Soviet Union, mainly because it was nothing of the sort, and did not try to be; we preferred to rely on other people's not-too-bright ideas instead of asserting our natural right to go our own sovereign way.

It is true that the radio and the newspapers in Moscow approved the January program of the Czechoslovak Party and said that it was the right way, a good way . . . but when they decided it was so much to their liking, how was it they said not a word all the time, expressed not a single doubt, disagreed with not a single aspect of the program followed all those years before January, almost twenty years?

It is not difficult to find the answer. They never "had any

trouble with Novotný," either problems to discuss or trouble of any other sort. There was trouble with Dubček from the outset. Dubček believed that Brezhnev and Kosygin really meant it when they talked of noninterference in the internal affairs of other countries, and therefore of other Socialist countries as well. He believed that after so many errors, it would be Soviet policy to abide by the principles so loudly proclaimed by their leaders, the principles of respect for state frontiers, state sovereignty, the immunity of the legal representatives of those states, the right to an independent Party program and an independent road to Socialism.

Because he trusted them he was dragged to Moscow in handcuffs.

In the course of time an interesting phenomenon developed in our Party. Someone would point out serious problems he did not have to invent because they were public knowledge. Out with him! Expel him from the Party! A year later the Party leaders would officially accept the fact that this particular problem was disturbing the whole country, would criticize it in the same terms as those used earlier by a more farsighted critic, and even take steps and prepare measures to deal with the problem; but nobody sent for the expelled comrade and said: you were right, forgive us for having misunderstood, it was a mistake. Here is your Party card back, and you can go back to your old job.

In Czechoslovakia, as in all the Socialist states, to be farsighted was absolutely forbidden. Naturally this led to the stagnation of public opinion, and the initiative of the ordinary citizens sank to naught.

A year ago I felt I had had enough of this. When the Israeli-Arab war broke out, there were signs that anti-Semitism was being officially revived, but that could have happened only if the hated government had given Israel the absolute support it gave the Arab countries instead. On the contrary, the policy of "unreserved support for the Arab countries" was a declaration of support for the plans to wipe out one small nation completely.

The censorship was by that time extremely tolerant on most questions, but the Arab-Israeli conflict roused the utmost vigilance. Not a word of doubt about our policy was allowed to appear in the press. Novotný broke off diplomatic relations with Israel about an hour after Brezhnev had done so.

It was just what Novotný wanted. Public opinion and the press were talking much too openly about the Slánsky trial and its consequences. Although he did not bear the major responsibility for the trial sometimes attributed to him, he was definitely mainly responsible for the 1954 trials, the trial of Husák and his group, and it was Novotný who saw to it that the innocent men and women victims were never given the public satisfaction demanded for them, in spite of the fact that the Party leadership itself called their trials a violent distortion of justice, a shocking infringement of the principles of Socialist justice, and even a crime.

In the course of its history, Novotný's regime was forced to make more than one change, more than one reform, but he never undertook anything of the sort on his own initiative. Every step forward was decided at the last moment, when public pressure was too great to resist, and often when it was too late to save the situation.

The revival of the "Zionist threat" was just what Novotný needed. Now he could postpone and silence the awkward questions that journalists, writers, and also workers were asking more and more openly and more and more insistently.

As late as 1963 he shouted: "The trials are never going to be discussed again!"

Yet a year later they were discussed, and by him, forced by public opinion to discuss them in a new way, condemning them. He talked of "newly discovered facts which were not known before," but he had been forced to bring the subject out into the open.

Who was this remarkable man with the remarkable career behind him, the subject for years of such jokes as:

"An empty Tatra 603 stopped in the Castle courtyard and the President of the Republic got out," and:

"There's a ghost walking around Prague Castle these days. A man without a head."

Where did this remarkable career start?

It started in the grim, disastrous year 1952, soon after Party headquarters by the Powder Tower had been "de-Zionized." At a meeting of the Central Committee, one of whose members was the modest little secretary of the Prague Regional Committee, Antonín Novotný, Klement Gottwald happened to notice him. He interrupted what he was saying to call out:

"Tonda, you'll have to go to the Powder Tower; we're short of people there now."

That was how it was arranged, simply and casually, a career such as would never have occurred to him in his wildest dreams. To such a trick of chance the Czechoslovak people owed the blessing that came to them in the shape of Antonín Novotný.

The Fifth

They do not know, in the manor house, that we do not sleep there. Soon after supper we all say good night and go to our rooms, and then leave by the back door. Yesterday a young worker from the village came to see me in the evening; I had never seen him in my life before.

"You ought not to sleep here at night," he said. "Here's a key to my cottage. My wife and I are going to her parents' place to sleep." I thanked him and he took me to his newly built cottage; it was big enough for the four of us, but they thought we'd rather be on our own.

This evening he came with two bottles of vodka. Hannah went to bed and we sat on in the kitchen. I didn't feel like drinking, but when a Slovak wants you to drink with him, there's no way of resisting.

We listened to the radio. They were adding still more transmitters to the legal network. The announcer said that President Svoboda, who had gone to Moscow to negotiate, was in the Kremlin, and that Dubček and the others they had arrested and taken off "to an unknown destination" had joined him.

"He shouldn't have gone there," my host said.

"What else could he do? He had to try to break down the vacuum in some way or other. He's probably saved those men's lives for them, and that's something."

"Do you think they'll manage anything?"

I shook my head. There was nothing they could hope to manage.

"Perhaps the Russians will back down. It didn't work out the way they wanted it, so perhaps they'll back down."

"They can't back down now. Once they decided to take such a step, they must have considered it in all its aspects and counted on the consequences the occupation of Czechoslovakia was bound to have."

"They didn't count on us—the way we've stuck together against them."

"That's nothing for them. They've got plenty of time; they've got the power in their hands and they can afford to have strong nerves. It's an unequal fight, and we haven't got either time or power or strong nerves on our side. And I don't know of anyone ready to stand by us, really help us. The world will wash its hands of us."

The radio announced that nearly eighty people had died and hundreds had been wounded so far, in Czech and Slovak towns, as a result of firing by the occupation forces.

"They haven't found anybody willing to be on their side."

"They haven't found anyone yet, but they will. Life goes on, and that means a certain degree of order. Somebody has got to run public affairs, our civilian life, and whoever it is will have to take them into account—they're here, they'll interfere in everything, and there's nothing that can be done about it. All they have to do is block their broad-gauge line to Čierna, or turn a stopcock on the pipeline, and there's no way we can get anything through from other countries, either. Nobody can stop them, there's nobody powerful enough."

"Does that mean we're at their mercy?"

"We've been at their mercy for a long time, only it wasn't so obvious."

"They can starve us out."

"They can, and if the worst comes to the worst, they may do it, if they can't get what they want any other way. And then people will work with them just to get bread, or at least that's what they'll say they're doing."

"Don't you see any other hope for us? Suppose they admitted they'd made a mistake, and retreated again."

No, I shook my head. I could not see any other hope, even if they did admit their mistake. The Twentieth Congress had ad-

mitted terrible mistakes indeed, and the occasion was meant to
serve as a protection against such things happening again. Such
confessions can be trusted only once; if you repeat them, they
no longer seem genuine.

"Suppose they retreat from our territory? They've shown us
they can roll their tanks across the whole country in a few hours.
Once they've done that, where is the guarantee they won't do it
again whenever they feel like it?"

The announcer was repeating an order by the Minister of the
Interior, Pavel, dismissing his deputy Viliam Šalgovič and taking
over the secret police himself.

"What are you going to do?"

"I don't know yet."

"You're afraid of the Russians, aren't you?"

"I am afraid of them."

"You should have gone by now."

"They haven't started arresting people yet, and it doesn't look
as though they are going to start soon. It looks as though they
aren't going to make the arrests themselves; they'll leave that to
our men borrowed for the purpose."

Before I left for Vietnam, one of the *Plamen* editors asked
me for an interview. The first question he asked was put like
this: Do you think that if a man in power thought it necessary
to gouge the eyes out in all newborn babies, there would be
three men in the world who would be willing and able to do
such a thing? My answer was that there would be, and far more;
there would be as many as the "operation" called for.

"The Russians are particularly interested in you, aren't they?"

"There's still time to decide to leave."

"You might fall into their clutches by some silly mistake. That
can happen, can't it?"

I had to admit it might happen.

"What would they do to you? Stage a trial?"

"Not at the moment. They wouldn't find anyone to run that
sort of a trial here, now."

That was Job's comfort. Imre Nagy and other victims of their
intervention were shot, it seems, long before they were said to

be coming up for trial. Beria is reported to have been shot at a meeting of the Executive Committee of the Communist Party of the Soviet Union by General Moskalenko. Two weeks later Tass issued a report that he had been tried for espionage and treason, and executed. If the struggle for power had been won by Beria instead of the others, which could quite well have happened, he would have accused his opponents of exactly the same crimes.

"You'll go abroad, won't you? You won't be able to write here; they won't let you publish. Even if they didn't put you in jail, they wouldn't let you earn a living."

"I don't know yet. I suppose we'll go abroad."

"Won't they call it a proof of treason and counterrevolution?"

"Sure, they will! The Poles have already started calling me a Zionist agent. I don't even have to emigrate."

"You aren't a Jew, though, are you?"

"No, I'm not, though it's been said of me for the third time now. That doesn't mean a thing. You don't necessarily have to be a Jew to be a Zionist agent; such people do exist."

The announcer told us that the Extraordinary Fourteenth Congress of the Communist Party of Czechoslovakia had met and taken a unanimous stand in support of Alexander Dubček and his policy, elected a new Central Committee with Dubček at its head, approved the new Party rules, and declared itself in permanent session, able to resume discussion of the agenda at any time. There were 1,280 delegates present, more than two-thirds of the number elected, and so the quorum was assured.

"Nobody's going to blame you if you stay abroad somewhere. Others may be blamed but not you."

"They'll blame me all right. You may blame me yourself, when you hear all the 'truths' about me they'll 'discover.' It happened before, just before I came back from Israel. Colleagues who knew me well passed a resolution that I was an anarchist, adventurer, exhibitionist, trying to keep in the limelight whatever the cost."

"Did you mind?"

"No, I didn't mind. When I read the statement made by the

Slovak Writers' Union and they asked me to reply, I said I
would rather be an anarchist and adventurer than the obedient
tool of those unworthy to hold power."

I considered the opportunities open to me. I could hide in the
mountains; there were people who would hide me and I'd have
no fear of betrayal. Friends offered me a comfortable cottage on
one of the innumerable islands in the Danube, where I could
probably never be found. There were plenty of very varied possi-
bilities. But what would be the point? Some people could start
preparing for illegal underground work against the occupation
forces; they could get together an underground group of Party
leaders ready for the worst if it should come, but there was
nothing I could do. I was too well known to too many people;
I would be a danger to those in the conspiracy with me. But to
wander about for months and even years in the mountains and
let myself be caught, sooner or later, as they would catch everyone; that was not a tempting prospect. At least not yet. I would
wait and see how things turned out. There would still be plenty
of time for Hannah and me to make up our minds. Not to make
up our minds, for whatever I pretended to myself I had really
made up my mind. But there would be time to carry out my
decision then. I had no intention of going like a lamb to the
slaughter.

"You've lived a year in exile already."

"Not quite. It was ten months, and I wasn't an *émigré*. I had
left the country legally, and it was the Czechoslovak Government that broke the law when it took away my Czechoslovak
citizenship, contrary to the law of the country."

"It's said an exile's life is a bitter one."

"I suppose it is. I never once fell into that mood, though, so
I can't say how bitter it tastes."

"But you'll be trying it out?"

"I suppose I'll be trying it out."

"Will you still be a Communist? Will you go on working for
the cause?"

"I shall still be a Communist. I shall be working for the cause, though I do not think anyone in exile will have the slightest hope of changing things."

"Why do you still want to be a Communist, after so many disappointments?"

"I don't know. It's somewhere very deep inside; it's the meaning of my whole life. It wasn't Stalin made me a Communist, nor Brezhnev, nor Novotný. It was my experience, my fighting temperament, my education, my feelings. I don't think I shall be alone; there are Communists all over the world who think the same as I do, and take the same view of the crime that has been committed here."

"Suppose it was Communism that has let us down? Maybe the goal we set ourselves is one that can never be reached."

"That may be, but neither you nor I can know, as yet. Even if it failed in the Soviet Union, even if it went absolutely bankrupt there, it still wouldn't mean it was unattainable. Maybe if the world had let us go on, we would have made something of Socialism in Czechoslovakia, something worthy of the name, something that would have attracted others. Perhaps that's the reason the West is so indifferent to what has happened to us."

"It's all to the good for them if the Socialist countries quarrel among themselves."

"It wouldn't matter to them if it wasn't that the Soviet Union gets stronger and more aggressive as she deserts the principles of Marx and Lenin. Socialism will undoubtedly be weaker after what has happened, but the Soviet Union has pushed her strategic frontiers nearer the West."

From the receiver came the news that the Italian Communist Party Executive Committee had sharply condemned the occupation of Czechoslovakia.

"It's not so long since you wrote that Czechoslovakia is not Santo Domingo."

"Czechoslovakia is still not Santo Domingo, but now the first Socialist great power is more of a great power than it is Socialist."

"This won't make any difference to Socialism in the Soviet Union, though."

"That's just it; it won't make any difference. And there's a great deal that needs changing there, practically everything. To make it real Socialism."

"You have no right to say that. Socialism doesn't have to be just the way you imagine it."

"That's true enough. Indeed it needn't be just the way Marx himself imagined it in his day. But while the world cannot agree on what Socialism should really be like, I think we can certainly agree on some things it should not and must not be allowed to be. A Socialist state cannot stand against its people; if it is to be a Socialist state, it must stand behind its people and be there for its people. Socialism must show itself more capable of solving the problems that arise in every healthy society, must offer a more dignified solution of them than previous systems have done. If it does not, it has no right to exist, and sooner or later it will degenerate and die out."

"What then? What happens after it has died out? Just nothing?"

"I don't know. Personally I think Socialism is man's last hope. But it needn't be so. Maybe our society has no hope left at all, and perhaps it has a hope of which we know nothing, something we haven't even guessed at. I don't mind what it is, if it creates bearable conditions and makes it possible for humanity to develop in a worthy manner, the whole of humanity without distinctions. So far nothing I have considered offered better prospects than Socialism. It could have been done by Christianity, but it was not and now is never likely to be. The unequal development of technical progress in different parts of the world offers no solution to our problems; technical progress itself is only a means, not a philosophy and not a god, though that is what people often mistake it for. The goal must be humanity, but so far we have had too little of it. That was what we were just trying to work out . . . that was what made the whole world watch what we were doing. And that was what the Soviet Union wanted to prevent."

"I wonder why?"

"Nobody knows the Russians' real motives; we can only guess

at them. We know very little about them today, much less than we did in the days of Khrushchev or Stalin. We don't even know who is the real ruler today, whether it's Brezhnev, or Yakubovsky, or somebody else whose name we have never even heard. All we know is that, for some internal or external political reason unknown to us, they decided to drop the principles of internationalism and equality among nations, which for years have been the most attractive thing about their policy."

"Maybe they're having trouble with their own people."

"It's possible. But they'd know what to do about them; they've always known."

"Do you think West Germany is really a genuine threat?"

"No, I don't. Today West Germany cannot get together the forces necessary to be a menace to the world. There are other countries, some of them much smaller, that have got much further ahead in spite of West Germany's great technical progress."

"They want to get hold of East Germany, though."

"They do that. All the fuss that's made by the revanchists and about the revanchists by the other side is ridiculous. But the moment the eastern and the western parts of Germany are made one, the strategical situation in Europe would change completely."

"That works both ways. To join West Germany to East Germany and put the whole under Ulbricht with Soviet control would be a great change in Europe. The other countries would not need to be occupied to realize that they now had an invincible neighbor."

"That's true. Especially if the Soviet Union managed to get the United States to disengage itself from Europe."

"Was our development a danger for East Germany, these last six months? Were they afraid of our democratization measures?"

"Maybe they were, but it was a bad calculation. They are not going to be able to press Socialism on the people by force forever. The moment they have the chance the East Germans are going to join the West Germans. The occupation of Czechoslovakia has only weakened the position of the East German Government."

"They can't do anything, anyway, as long as the Soviet occupation army is there."

"Not for the time being. It's a question what sort of Socialism they've got that has to be enforced by the army. Socialism will be O.K. in East Germany when it doesn't need a single soldier to keep it in power, when it's so much to the liking of the people that they want to defend it of their own accord. Ulbricht's policy is doing more to destroy it than to make it popular."

The radio announced that in Prague, although no curfew had been officially imposed, Soviet soldiers were shooting at everything that moved in the streets in the evening. The reporter at the microphone told what he had seen: the Soviet soldiers shot at an ambulance, and refused to allow help for the wounded lying in the street. There were dead bodies lying there. Soviet tanks had shot up the terrace and facade of the National Museum and gunners were practicing marksmanship on the statue of St. Wenceslas at the top of the Square.

My host said: "Drink it up yourself; I'd better get to bed. I have to get up early for work in the morning," and went out. I was left alone with the unfinished bottle of vodka. It was good of him to come.

The news coming over the air was pretty grim, but we had been sitting over a bottle of vodka, talking about Socialism. Where else in the world, I reflected, would that have been possible? Not many places, I thought.

I was alone, and the vodka did me good. . . .

In 1962 a correspondent of the American Associated Press came to see me, to ask about developments in Slovakia.

I asked if he was permanently accredited to Czechoslovakia; he did not hide his amusement.

"Oh, no, I'm the regular correspondent in Vienna. There's nothing going on here, you know; it would be an extravagance to keep an office going."

There was "nothing going on here." Of course there was nothing going on. We were living through the apparently calm years of Novotný's bureaucratic dictatorship. In his view, and that of Western Europe, we were not allowed to write or even to talk in private of what we really thought. We were all loud-speakers for his official propaganda. We were the firmest bastion of Stalinism in Eastern Europe.

There were visible signs of democratization in the country, however. The terror had practically ceased, and even in the press there was more opportunity to vent opinions. About 1964 the foreign correspondents in Czechoslovakia were as thick as flies. "Something" seemed to be moving. A young reporter from the Vienna *Die Presse* came and asked me for an interview, saying that he was actually a music critic. I agreed, and he took out a small tape recorder. I answered his questions, and it was a lot of fun. I tried to explain to him very patiently what was behind the social changes taking place, the root of our "intellectual opposition," but he wasn't really very interested. He kept switching the thing on and off according to what he wanted to record. What he wanted to record was his own idea of things in Czechoslovakia and of me personally.

The article about me came out a few days later in *Die Presse,* entitled: "An Intellectual Rebel or a Party Spy?"

That same year I took part in a Vienna-Prague television discussion, and mentioned this article as an example of the insensitive treatment of our problems by the Western press. I happened to run into the same reporter in 1967, and he recorded another short interview, saying in the introduction that I had been angry with him for having, in my view, distorted our earlier talk.

Well, we were prepared for such experiences; in the course of time we had grown accustomed to that sort of reporting. But in spite of these distortions, the world slowly began to find out that we were doing something and aiming at something. We wanted the world to know.

More or less "invisibly" to Western eyes, we had been preparing our invisible 1968 revolution. The world sharpened its senses. What had happened to Czechoslovakia all at once? Always so obedient, where had that sudden will, that determination, come from? It doesn't matter. What we were doing was not being done for the sake of the West, but for our own sake.

Even so, the insensitive Western press did not help us much; in fact it was an illusion to think the correspondents could help us much. Their lack of understanding of the real inner context and their constant references to a handful of intellectuals who had succeeded in ousting Novotný and turning Czechoslovak policy in another direction only served to provide the Soviet with ammunition for the fight against "revisionism and against counterrevolutionary elements in the shape of certain journalists, artists and writers."

In confirmation of their thesis, the Soviet propaganda chiefs have only to quote any Western paper. Is not this what the bourgeois press of the West is writing with some malice? Do they not say exactly what the Moscow *Pravda* says?

The legend that the intellectuals revolted against Novotný is still widely believed in the Western world as almost the only explanation of the events of the spring of 1968 in Czechoslovakia. Yet it is absurd. Nowhere in the world can a group of intellectuals, whatever their program, introduce fundamental political changes unless society is ripe for these changes, unless they fit in with the views and wishes of the public.

It was not the intellectuals who got rid of Novotný, but the fact that the vast majority of the people knew that the country was in a state of long-drawn-out economic, political and moral crisis, that we had got into a blind alley, and that we would have to act differently unless we wanted complete catastrophe. All the intellectuals did was to articulate this spontaneous public feeling and to express the ideas and wishes of the people.

The people had realized that without the opportunity for individual initiative society as a whole cannot move forward, but the necessary conditions for this initiative to develop were missing. There was no freedom guaranteeing the right to have ideas without the risk that they would be distorted and made the excuse for political persecution. The leveling down of salaries and wages meant that a situation developed that can best be expressed by the current Czechoslovak joke that people are paid for being in a job and not paid for doing a job. The elastic social laws were more help to the idlers and ruffians than to the decent, hard-working citizen. There was no penalty, especially among workers, for careless, bad work, laziness, or sharp practice. There are jokes which are almost proverbial, so well do they depict the dangerous state of affairs:

"If you don't rob the state you are robbing your own family."
Or:

"If you hesitate, you'll go hungry."

Even if it was possible to get rid of someone who was lazy, inefficient, or dishonest, he could laugh in everyone's faces, for he would easily find another and better job, easier and better paid.

And he did. These sins against working morale were of no importance; all that mattered was that one have the "right class origin."

What was the "right class origin"? The first and best was a working-class origin, and next came a peasant origin. A third class origin to confess to was that of a state official's family, a doctor or an engineer—in a word, the bourgeois intelligentsia. In the case of the Jews, this class racialism ceased to be purely a matter of class.

It was not so important for parents; they were what they were and not always what they were supposed to be. But it was of prime importance in getting into a university. It was not until 1964 that the class criteria were abolished in the selection of future students.

But what exactly was meant by, say, a peasant origin? Many a peasant was marked down as a kulak because he did not want to join a farming cooperative. And what was working-class origin? Part of the bourgeoisie emigrated after February, 1948, but most of them stayed in the country. What happened to them? They were "reeducated" either free or in prison, and emerged as crane drivers, asphalt layers, ironworkers, miners, quarrymen. In 1963 the son of any of these men could write "working class" in the space on his application marked "Class Origin." Rightly. Whatever way you looked at it, his father was a worker. But since 1948 a new intelligentsia had grown up from the old working class, in accelerated secondary-school courses, in courses for teachers' diplomas, for engineering degrees, for officers' rank. The son of a former worker who had been a high army officer for over ten years, or a university lecturer (and there were some) or an engineer or a factory manager—could he say he was a worker's son? The question to be answered referred to the present occupation of the applicant's father.

Thus the son of a former factory owner now turned worker had the advantage over the son of a worker turned engineer—perhaps from the same factory. It always angered me from the true class point of view; it made no sense.

A well-known university professor came to see me, angry and upset. For class reasons his daughter had been refused admission to the faculty where he himself lectured.

Political crimes—a concept that is not fixed, precisely defined, and often not even proved—were placed on the same level or even a higher level of significance than that of crime proper, and this obliterated the dividing line between the two and often reversed their relative importance. Ernest Otta was condemned to death for having in his library the Constitution of Tito's Yugoslavia; Ladislav G. was condemned to death for political sabotage; yet at this time convicted murderers, who in many countries and previously in Czechoslovakia, too, would have been punished only by death, were being given sentences of fifteen or ten years' imprisonment.

It was only logical that in such a system of justice the moral aspect of punishment disappeared. Swindlers, embezzlers, those who stole state property, were all considered "political victims of the regime."

During the First Republic, a postman whom I knew could not account for eight hundred crowns he had to deliver that day, when there was a spot check on him. It was useless for him to swear that he had only borrowed the money because he needed it urgently and would repay it in three days. He had committed a precisely defined offense and got two months' imprisonment. But when he came out of jail, he could never be a postman again and his former colleagues would have nothing to do with him. After February, 1948, this moral concomitant disappeared from punishment for offenses. Today a postman might not even be convicted for this offense, for example, if he were an active Communist. But if they did bring him to court, he would get several years, in the knowledge that he would actually serve half of it. On his release he could reapply for the job of postman and would probably get it again. And his former colleagues? They would probably welcome him back with a smile, and if they said anything about his offense at all, it would be: Bad luck . . . never mind, it can happen to all of us.

Naturally all the advantages are on the side of the habitual criminal in our prisons. And it is grotesque to read of a restaurant manager caught in flagrant defrauding of the public, or a shop manager, and being given a sentence in which the judge literally makes a point of the fact that the prisoner is not to follow his profession during the duration of his sentence.

The honest workers were at a disadvantage, regarded with mistrust by their fellows. They "spoiled" norms, or "got to the top by stepping on us." More than once such "undesirable" behavior has been rewarded fist-wise.

I went into the case of the manager of a restaurant who tried to work and live honestly, which was not to the liking of the supply firms, the district manager of the restaurant business, and various other interested parties who formed a widespread gang of thieves in a certain North Bohemian district. The manager got five years' imprisonment, on the basis of falsified accounts arranged by these men. It was a difficult job to get the sentence quashed on the grounds of illegality. And nothing at all happened to the people who had framed him; for all I know they are hard at work stealing still.

As long as we were living on capital, as long as the state finances could meet all the foolish losses caused by the production of useless goods that went from the workshop straight to the scrap heap—as in the Tesla plant in Hradec Králové, in the Brno engineering works, and certainly elsewhere as well, if not almost everywhere—we managed to get along. But no society can last forever with such husbandry, and in 1960, the year that

Czechoslovakia officially became a Socialist republic, sharp disparities began to appear in the market, in wages, in prices, and in working morale, and tension grew. People began to think about what was going on, why things were so, and who was to blame. The system had exhausted the supply of scapegoats and there were no more hostile isms to blame. Nobody would believe that sabotage could be carried out on such a vast scale by one individual or even a group of individuals. All at once the cause of our stagnation was clear and familiar to all—the saboteur, a gigantic one, was the inefficiency and stupidity of the bureaucratic system.

The long invisible crisis came out into the open suddenly, so suddenly that the Prime Minister (it was Široký at the time) let an unguarded remark slip into one of his speeches. . . . "I cannot understand how it is possible; I do not know what has happened to our economy."

The Prime Minister did not know and did not understand what the whole nation knew by then, what intellectuals had been saying for years. Although during the trials the workers had not been very concerned—after all, the accused were intellectuals living on the workers who were being got rid of—they suddenly began to see the connection between the terror and the growing economic crisis.

Not just a few intellectuals. It was the discontented working class that forced the revolutionary changes in the system of management of industry and also in the staffing of high positions in the state and the Party. It was an economic crisis Novotný's system did not know how to deal with, one which got worse after every promised measure to improve it, that did the trick. The intellectuals only formulated and documented these facts.

Since the time of the Twentieth Congress of the Communist Party of the Soviet Union, a quiet and underground but nevertheless very-well-thought-out struggle had been going on in Czechoslovakia, to achieve a different method of running the country and the Party. What happened in Hungary had slowed down this struggle and made it more difficult, but had not stopped it altogether. A nationwide discussion ensued, long-drawn-out and passionate, more and more open and angry; intellectuals gave it expression in their writings, films, and works of art. The nation realized that the crisis was primarily a moral one, the consequence and not the cause of which was the economic stagnation of the country. The nation was looking for an explanation and a way out.

The ever more outspoken and critical discussion to be seen in the newspapers was only one-tenth of the iceberg, its visible part.

In Czechoslovakia the relations between the state and the administration, and between the leaders of the administration and the people, were very involved. The people were anxious to preserve Socialism and were anxious about the fate of Socialism; so much was being done slowly and hesitantly because haste and impetuosity might endanger Socialism altogether. But what the people meant by the word was not what their self-instituted leaders meant. When public opinion reached this stage, the departure of Novotný from the scene, along with his absurd bureaucratic system, was only a matter of time. A longer or a shorter time, that was not the point. The important thing was what would take the place of this system. Out of the frying pan into the fire was no solution.

Is there any need to give proof of this, after what happened in Czechoslovakia in 1968? The tremendous popular feeling "for Dubček," the fantastic unity of the whole nation, provides the best proof. It was not a question of Dubček himself, but of his program of democratization. Dubček was neither the author nor the instrument, nor the sole guarantor of the program, but he was its symbol.

The intellectuals, feeling victorious, were not sure on one point. They could not be sure of the workers' reactions. Dubček did not follow Churchill's example and promise blood, sweat, and tears, but every one of his listeners felt it. Would the working class, which the intelligentsia felt was bound to be demoralized by the past years, stand up to this sacrifice demanded of it? For things to take a turn for the better, they would have to get worse, suddenly, sharply, and everywhere, but especially in the standard of living. We had eaten the state out of house and home, and now we would have to pay for it. In February of this strange year, Novotný was still active, rousing the workers of the biggest engineering plant in Prague—there you are, you see, that's what comes of it all! Conditions are deteriorating fast. . . .

If the intellectuals had been in closer contact with the working class and had known better what the workers really thought about things, much could have been done sooner and more rapidly. I would even go so far as to say that, if the working class had been more deeply committed to the regeneration program, the worst need not have happened.

It's too late now to start looking for the mistakes. It happened, and today it is the working class above all that stands behind Dubček while a censorship dictated by the Soviet authorities is imposing silence on the intellectuals, and they are preparing for another inner emigration.

The threat to the democratization process did not come from within, but from a direction where nobody expected it, carried by the tanks of the Soviet Army.

During the past ten years I have had many opportunities to discuss our problems with friends and enemies abroad. We have discussed freedom. Democracy. Freedom for art and literature. For the press. Responsibility. I have talked all night in private, spoken at public meetings and debates, and written in the Western press. I always refused to take up the defensive position into which our Western partners tried to press us. Democracy, yes, but where do you see it? Where can you point to democracy? Which nation has the good fortune to possess it? The consumer society of West Germany? American democracy with its war of extermination in Vietnam? Or De Gaulle's French democracy? The two or more party system is no guarantee of democracy, I argued; they can always form a "great coalition"; nor does the subjection of members of the National Assembly to Party discipline guarantee that the people have the best representatives.

What kind of democracy? What kind of freedom? While the people in one-half of the globe are working, those in the other half, the antipodal half, are asleep. Somewhere, on some line of latitude, of longitude, there is a pentagonal building, and in it a group of men bound to silence. They sit over a map of the world and draw lines across it. What are their lines for? Destruction. The enemy may attempt this, and we shall answer thus. Half humanity is fast asleep, never dreaming that a line has just been drawn through them, that their death has just been decided, and that the date is nearer now. Secret diplomacy, military secrecy, the immoral agreement between the two atom powers to prevent the bombs coming into the possession of other nations. The young people of America are demonstrating, but the filthy, aggressive war of extermination is still carried on in Vietnam. The Soviet Union keeps on arousing the Arab nations against the small state of Israel, which has done nothing to them and cannot threaten their strategic interests. If you were to ask the nations whether they want it this way, the answer would be an overwhelming no! Nobody wants it. But the politicians, under the cloak of diplomatic secrecy, military and state secrecy, continue to have their way.

Politics are out of date, clinging to methods evolved in and suitable for the nineteenth century and of no use in our very different age.

Up to now no war has really wiped out its victims; even if decimated, the defeated have survived as a nation and recovered. The war to come will be different, will wipe out nations, yet the decision is left at the mercy of political systems subservient to the way of thinking of the past.

One of the forms taken by the lack of freedom in the Socialist countries is the habit of making everything "top secret." Insofar as the terror had any purpose, it was to keep things secret, to guard state secrecy. Democracy would thus be a system in which nothing was secret, nothing was kept hidden from the people, a system in which political terror would have no point.

Where is such a system to be found? Where is there a government run on those lines? Where is that democracy? The one-eyed is no less one-eyed for putting himself above the blind.

Is there a fortunate country where there are no state secrets and no terror? That terror is not visible does not mean it is nonexistent.

The threat to the world is too serious for us to put our common fate into the hands of "seven wise men," whether in Moscow, Peking, or Washington, in good faith that they will do their best. They talk of peace, of the need to improve relations, but in the safe at General Headquarters, they each have a set of perfectly worked out plans for the destruction of the others.

This is the century of the generals. The generals of whom Clemenceau once said: "A general? Isn't that something that was once a colonel?"

Generals are superfluous in peacetime and suffer from the schizophrenia of their position. A general is great only on the field of battle. What general does not long to be great and famous? An American general? A Soviet general? But once we are agreed that this is the century of generals (of course we may be wrong), then we ought to agree on the rest—that any discussion of democracy is useless, for the nations of the world are subject to military discipline. Today the meaning of democracy ought to merge with that of humanity, but neither the Americans nor the Soviet authorities have attempted to prove their right to a leading position in the world by showing their humanity. They do it by a show of force. And since they fear a contest of power with one another, they prove their strength against the small nations: Israel, Vietnam, Czechoslovakia . . .

I feel that democracy ends where the citizen of one country is brought before a military tribunal for refusing to fight, say, in Vietnam, because to do so goes against his conscience and beliefs. It ends where a citizen of the Soviet Union is beaten up in Red Square and brought before a tribunal for protesting against the occupation of Czechoslovakia. It ends where a citizen of any country can be charged with treason for refusing to drop an atom bomb on the towns of another country. At this limit of humanity there is no choice, in any country of the world. In the political vocabulary, freedom still means destroying, limiting, and suppressing the freedom of the individual and of whole nations. In Santo Domingo in the name of one set of ideals, in Czechoslovakia in the name of another set. And in Tibet. And in Biafra. The freedom of the great is the freedom of violence done to the weak.

I, as a Communist, was free to protest against the freedom to commit violence enjoyed by the United States, Great Britain, or France. I was free to protest to my heart's content, and was approvingly slapped on the back for it.

I was even free to protest about some things going on inside the Czechoslovak Socialist Republic. I got no approving slaps on the back for it, but at least it was becoming more and more possible. Little of what I have mentioned in this book had not already appeared over my name in books or articles, and not only in the last six months, but particularly up to 1964.

Yet even I, all these years, had kept to a taboo I had imposed on myself. The taboo subject was the foreign policy and internal policy of the Soviet Union. Up to January, 1968, nobody would have printed anything I wrote on the subject, but I did not even try.

The aspects of Soviet policy that I did not like I explained away as the result of awkwardness, lack of experience, inconsistency on the part of the young, undeveloped Socialist Great Power, menaced on all sides by hostile countries. The errors, I felt, were formal and not fundamental.

For years I was convinced of the justice of the Moscow trials, thanks to the evidence of an unbiased observer, the American ambassador to Moscow, Joseph Davies, whose book *Mission to Moscow* was trustworthy evidence when others were not.

The pact with Hitler was a cynical, frightening thing, but it could be explained by the need to gain time for the essential preparations for the life-and-death struggle ahead.

The occupation of the Baltic republics and part of Poland, and the war against Finland, were excused by the subsequent victory over Fascist Germany. It was not the desire for expansion but strategic necessity that dictated Stalin's policy, and the outcome of the war confirmed this.

After the Second World War the Soviet Union never intervened openly in other countries, with the exception of Hungary, not even where Socialist countries were in open conflict with American imperialism in Korea and Vietnam.

Conditions in Hungary were very involved. In Budapest armed rebels were killing Soviet soldiers who were stationed in the country by the terms of the peace treaty and other valid agreements. The Soviet Army intervened at the request of one of the two parties involved in the struggle. It was not possible to swallow this explanation whole, and it chilled the spine, but it was accepted as an explanation by people who did not want to admit that the Socialist Great Power was willing to trample underfoot the principles by which she stood.

For nearly ten years the Hungarian question remained on the agenda of the United Nations. How many of the acts of violence perpetrated by the United States even were put on the agenda? Guatemala? Intervention against the Greek partisans? Panama? Santo Domingo? Lebanon? The unsuccessful invasion of Cuba? Its aggression in Vietnam? The countries that blamed the Soviet Union for Budapest were involved before that year was out in an irresponsible military adventure in Suez, later sent white mercenaries into Katanga, tried to exterminate the Algerian people; for twenty years they have been fighting in Vietnam in one constellation or another. They accuse the Soviet Union of staging Communist revolutions in Poland, Hungary, Romania, Bulgaria, and Czechoslovakia, but they themselves have inspired and supported reactionary officers' revolutions in Europe, Asia, Africa, and Latin America.

Compared with the armed intervention of the United States in the internal affairs of many countries, the "Hungarian question," although disturbing, seemed doubtful, to say the least.

At the time when the war in Vietnam was being stepped up, it was Kosygin's initiative that brought the war between India and Pakistan to an end. The numerous statements by Soviet politicians that their country was pursuing a policy of peace sounded, against the background of world developments, far more genuine than similar declarations from the United States.

The Soviet Union had almost convinced her nearer and farther neighbors that her peace policy was meant in earnest, that she really respected her international agreements and did not intend to interfere in the internal affairs of other countries, respecting their sovereignty—in spite of Hungary and her intervention there in 1956. After the incident was over, the Soviet withdrew her troops except for those agreed on under the peace treaty and the bilateral agreements between the two countries.

Those who compare developments in Czechoslovakia today with what happened in Hungary then are wrong. The Soviet troops, who have no business in Czechoslovakia, will not be withdrawn. In Hungary the Soviet authorities allowed a certain measure of liberalization in public life, but in Czechoslovakia they will not allow the liberalization and democratization to continue, for it was precisely these tendencies that decided the question of invasion at all.

By the occupation of Czechoslovakia, the Soviet Government lost once and for all its reputation as peacemakers and guardians of international principles and conventions.

No one will ever again trust Soviet assurances, believe its promises; smiles will arouse increased vigilance, a proffered hand will be regarded with fear.

I have had the bitter, joyless satisfaction of having revealed the "true face of Moscow" a year ago, having gone where I could be heard in order to protest against this policy, having rebelled against it before ever it gave any sign of threatening the sovereignty of my own country, and rebelled somewhat sooner than other European and Czechoslovak Communists. I had passionate arguments with Italian Communists about Israel's "aggression," for they were still unreservedly supporting the foreign policy of the Soviet Union. Democratic developments in Czechoslovakia helped the Italian Communists toward their election victory, and there is no need to stress what their attitude toward Soviet foreign policy is today; it is well known. Half a year ago they shouted me down when I talked of the great power strategy of the Soviet Union, which was not yet clear to everyone in spite of the presence of a strong Soviet naval force in the Mediterranean.

What was not clear then has now become quite clear.

The Communist parties of Western Europe are faced with a severe crisis. They will be able to repair their damaged reputations only insofar as they face up to the new situation, to the fact that Moscow was never sincere in her claims to be, is not, and never will be, the "guarantor and avant-garde of the world Socialist revolution," as Nikita Khrushchev claimed in 1958.

Communist internationalism has not died out, but in the Soviet Union it is in its last throes.

One of my friends, desperate at the thought of Soviet aggression against us, said to me: "They will regret it bitterly one day, and condemn what they have done." That is possible, indeed it is very likely—but what good will it do us? Will their belated self-criticism give us back the young people they murdered? Can human life be made up for by any explanations and excuses? Can trust be revived once it has been so crushed? Is it right, however far in the future, to build up new relationships on trust alone? Suppose they do retire now, suppose they all leave—a few weeks before the occupation they withdrew from our territory the forces they had here, and which had no right here. They went away—and in two weeks they were back again. Who is going to believe that they are going, never to return? Who in Czechoslovakia can ever trust them again in anything?

Maybe they think they can get along without our trust, now. So many have thought so before them. They have not yet learned that this is one of the last stages before the—end? An end which, in spite of everything that has happened, is not and cannot be a matter of indifference to me and my comrades? That although we are bitterly resentful of what they have done to us, we tremble for the fate of the Soviet Union itself?

Sooner or later, such a policy must end in utter catastrophe. It was not I, but a great Russian poet of long ago who cried: "Woe to thee, Russia!"

The
Sixth

Svoboda and Dubček have still not returned from Moscow and nobody knows when they will come back. People are afraid of what may happen to them, and resolutions demanding their immediate return are getting more and more frequent.

The fact that they have not yet come home can mean only one thing: they are still holding out. They have not yet given in, they are refusing to sign the conditions being forced on them under duress. What those conditions are it does not take much to guess. Several Soviet divisions to remain on our western frontier; the censorship to be established again; changes in the leading positions in the government and the Party. According to the people forced upon us by the Soviet authorities, we shall be able to judge them for what they are. In these dramatic, sad, and noble days the part each played in the past has been erased; there was nothing before the twentieth of August; those days are forgotten, forgiven, gone completely; nobody will be judged now by what he did or said then. Only action, deeds done now, will allow us to judge each man, even those we insulted for months as conservative, dogmatic Stalinists.

General Kodaj, who took such a violent stand against the authors of the "Two Thousand Words" and demanded the reintroduction of the censorship, has declared his support for Dubček and explained his previous position. Almost all the collaborators "exposed" as such have indignantly denied it, and proclaim their loyalty to Dubček and the Republic. Are they sincere? Nobody can tell. The radio calls constantly: no witch-hunting! Do not injure honest people by spreading suspicion; untold damage can be done to our greatest treasure—human beings. Indignantly the program condemned a schoolteacher who is said to have pilloried a child before the class because her father was accused of collaborating.

One reporter even got an interview with Novotný. Even Novotný, today, if he condemned the occupation and refused to have anything to do with it, would be given the respect and confidence he never enjoyed while in office. He did not. He declared that he had left political life to live in retirement. It is not much, these days, but even so the nation is grateful for that little. And so not even he invited the Soviet Army here to help him!

What days they were, what weeks, what months! A revolution for human dignity, a revolution against deformation of the human spirit, against arbitrary political action, and for common sense. That is something absolutely new. And this revolution will not lose its human face—indeed, it will show it even more clearly—even in days of the greatest trials to which human society is exposed.

The Russians are here, the occupation army; nothing is too good for anyone willing to go along with them, there are wonderful careers to be made for the asking, yet not a soul in the country is ready to lend himself to "gouge out the eyes of the newborn." For the first time in history there are no quislings. Six days after the occupation began, the Soviet authorities have still not found anyone to support them. This is a terrible political debacle, forcing them to the incredible declaration that they have not come to interfere in our internal affairs.

They have found no one and it does not look as though they will find anyone. And so they are forced to negotiate with Dubček.

I wonder what the negotiations look like. They are sitting at a big table, with Brezhnev on one side and Dubček and Svoboda on the other, and looking at each other across the table. How does Brezhnev feel—the man about whom a favorite joke among Czechoslovaks says that his bushy eyebrows are really only Stalin's moustaches on a higher level? What is his expression as he looks at the men he assured only fourteen days earlier that there could be no question of military intervention, that he fully supported the policy followed by the Czechoslovak Party after January?

How does he feel? He probably feels good. How does he look? He is probably laughing at them: you fell for it, you fools, we put a fast one over on you, naïve and stupid as you are; you believed what we said, you amateur politicians, dilettantes, nobodies, you did not see through my cat-and-mouse game. Čierna and Tisou? Bratislava? Nothing but a diplomatic trick, a political sell. That fraternal embrace was the kiss of Cain. Beg my pardon, Abel: repeat after me . . . sign here . . . a public statement . . . forgive me, Cain, for your having had to kill me.

You think he should be ashamed of himself? What for? For being so clever? You cannot ask that of him. He is ready to declare tomorrow, if need be, that Dubček is the finest son ever born to a Slovak mother. Sign, sign, time presses and every hour is precious. The world is stupid and uncomprehending, getting nervous as you delay. How can you hold things up so?

They will sign. Perhaps in an hour, perhaps in two hours . . . but they have not signed yet. They have not got so far. Svoboda has said he is returning to Prague this evening at the latest, with an agreement or without one.

They will sign that they agree to the presence of Soviet troops in Czechoslovakia, for there is nothing they can do about it once the troops are there. They will sign that they maintain the validity of the Warsaw Pact, of which they never had the slightest doubt anyway. And, above all, they will sign that the censorship will be reestablished.

The censorship . . . The fact that this demand is being pressed so vehemently shows only too clearly what the main objection was to the way things were going in Czechoslovakia. Why they really came, what it is they are most afraid of.

For half a year the Czechoslovak press had been absolutely free. What was so strange about that? It was only carrying out the relevant clause in the Constitution, similar to that valid in all the Socialist countries. This clause on civil liberties includes the guarantee of freedom of the press. There is nothing in the

Constitution to permit limitation of this freedom. In Czechoslovakia the censorship had no legal existence and the institution
carrying it out was called "aid." The censor did not have the
right to remove articles from the papers; he could only "advise"
the editor not to publish them. If the editor did not take his
advice, though, he would not put on the manuscript (which the
editor was bound to send to him) the little green stamp without
which the paper could not be printed.

The Czechoslovak National Assembly had declared this censorship to be illegal and unconstitutional, and passed a law for-
bidding it.

Dubček's crime was to try to govern strictly according to the
Constitution, according to law. For the first time in its history,
the Party group that won the leadership did not carry out a
"purge." Novotný went of his own accord when he realized his
position was untenable. They patiently tried to make him see he
was an obstacle to progress, to admit the tremendous damage he
had done and to draw the right conclusion. They could have decreed his retirement, they could have kicked him out the way
he kicked out the people he had overcome in the struggle for
power. Novotný did not go until he saw he was alone, deserted
even by his former favorites.

Dubček's crime was to proceed according to the strict pro-
visions of the law. The laws were elastic and full of holes and
not easy to take as a guide, but laws they were, and Dubček
thought they should be followed and respected by all.

Dubček's crime was to see his role as the servant of and not
the dictator to his people. He introduced the secret ballot into
Party elections, and it was to be adopted in parliamentary and
municipal elections, too. He thought nobody had the right to
hold his political position forever; the leaders should be those
who have the confidence of the people, and not chosen as Gottwald did Novotný: "Tonda, you'll have to go to the Powder
Tower." And they should serve only as long as they keep that
confidence by their policy. What a threat that would be to
Brezhnev!

Dubček's crime was his humanity. Thousands of innocently

wronged victims had the moral right to revenge, yet none demanded it. From time to time there would appear in the press an interview with a politician or public official, now out of public life, but known to have committed terrible crimes against humanity. An interview with the General Procurator in the Slánsky trial, Urválek. An interview with the Minister of Security at that time, Bacílek. An interview with one of the cruelest men in the security services, who had "interrogated" many accused, Doubek. It was like a dream; there was the reporter, cups of coffee, civilized questions. . . . How could you do it? How could you have thought it was right? What do you think of it all now? Yes, I did indeed do terrible things, I was as I am described. . . . There were interviews with the victims, and the surviving families of victims. . . .

The first condition was to tell the truth; when the truth is out, and not before, we can start to put things right. The hypocrisy and lies they had grown up listening to was what lay heaviest on the minds of the young people; it was a boulder they helped to roll away with enthusiasm. The clear honesty of these youngsters, their sense of outrage at the past, their readiness to work for something they felt they could at last have a say in—all that was in some way Dubček's crime, too.

They showed an amazing sense of responsibility; pouring in by thousands into the largest hall in Prague, their sheer weight damaged one of the iron doorways. Before the meeting was over, an eight-hour exchange of opinion with those who were coming forward to head the new trend in political life, the hat had gone around to make good the damage to the door.

There was a student demonstration against the war in Vietnam, sometime before, in front of the American Embassy; some Vietnamese students threw stones at the windows and tore down the American flag. Czech students demonstrating with them pressed them back, gathered up the dirty flag and took it into the building: we do not approve of your aggressive war in Vietnam, and we came to tell you so, loud, under your windows, for you to hear us. But we will not allow anyone to dishonor the flag of your great nation. We came here to protest, not to destroy like barbarians.

Oh, it was too good to be true!

It was too good to be true when the Minister of the Interior protested angrily at the treatment of the writer Ladislav Mňačko: "We have done something to be ashamed of, and we must make it good. It is in my power to restore his citizenship, and if anyone objects, then I'm in the wrong place and I'll resign. As long as I hold this office, the law is going to be kept. Or else I don't want to have anything to do with it."

It was too good to be true when the Czechoslovak Press Agency was empowered to state that there was not a single political prisoner in the state prisons.

I expected our revolution to be threatened from a different side. I said to myself it was too good to be true—but what for? What is the good of all this enthusiasm, hard work, wise endeavor? It is getting late, and the world is speeding to destruction. We cannot evade it. The H-bombs will fall on innocent and guilty alike, and if the world continues to become more and more cynical at the present rate, the end is not far off.

I was fourteen when Hitler came to power, a normal kid like all the working-class kids in our street. A tough customer, always ready for a fight—with one reservation. My father once caught me hitting a boy two years my junior; he taught me the lesson of my life.

"Never hit anyone weaker than yourself," he said; "hit the bigger ones, and always fight so they can't beat you."

In every respect except one I was absolutely normal, and that one unusual feature was my passion for politics. We had our own gang with our own leader, and we fought some pretty sharp battles. I never wanted to be the leader, but whenever I could I got them talking politics. As far as fourteen-year-olds can be said to have any political views, ours were clear and decided. We lived in a "Red" street, and we had to keep up our reputation. Our deadly enemy was the bourgeoisie, which we thought was the same thing as Fascism.

At sixteen I was sitting on the doorsteps with the grown workers, joining in their arguments. They listened to me attentively, never shutting me up for being too young and green.

From fourteen onward I had the feeling there was someone lying in wait to leap at my neck. The feeling was sometimes so intense that it amounted to physical fear. Even today if anyone puts a hand on the back of my neck, even in friendship, I lose my head and hit out, instinctively, with my fists. I can't help it, it's beyond the control of my reason.

From fourteen onward I was in the thick of things. For me Fascism came to mean my own destruction, and I decided not to give in to it, not to give in to anyone. I fought Fascism by word and deed and with arms. When Fascism was defeated, the feeling of physical menace hanging over me, the feeling that a knife was always whizzing by my ear, still did not leave me. There was the American policy of atomic blackmail, and I saw no other way of meeting that threat than the one proposed by the Communists. I went along with them, convinced that theirs was the only way to fend off destruction.

I still think so today, and I still go along with them.

I cannot be turned from this path by the shameful thing that has been done to my country. The dirty things we have done were done by the Hitler in us and had little to do with our humanistic ideals. A beast lies slumbering in us all, and in me. The beast woke and wrought its worst during the years of the terror. I thought it a Communist's duty to do everything to suppress and destroy the beast.

I rebelled. I rebelled somewhat sooner than many others did.

In 1953, when there was a tendency to anti-Semitic pogroms among Slovak writers, they were trying to drive out the only Jewish writer of any standing in Slovak literature at the time; I waved a red rag in front of the anti-Semitic bull, the first visible sign of my inner rebellion. The discussion that ensued in the newspaper lasted a year and a half. The elite of the Slovak writers took their stand against me and those who came to my support; on the surface the argument concerned the quality and significance of a not very successful novel, of which one of the critics said reproachfully that "the author shows in this book that he does not belong to the context of Slovak literature."

This was the sentence I attacked, and in the course of those eighteen months, the discussion narrowed down to the concepts that had been hovering in the background from the outset. We were only waiting for our antogonists to come into the open, and we were ready with our reply. We knew that sooner or later they would use the word cosmopolitanism, and that gave us our chance to reply with bourgeois nationalism, which was a dangerous accusation to make in Slovakia in those days. We won the long-drawn-out newspaper war, but the discussion did not stop there. It passed into other spheres and groupings, and is still going on today. It will not be without interest for the future literary historian to note that in Slovakia we did not have to wait for the Twentieth Congress. In *Kulturný Život* for 1955 there are many articles by various writers, dealing with the moral aspects of the deformations of Marxism. I was always in the vanguard of those rousing informed opinion.

In 1951 I wrote a play, *Bridges to the East*. Today it could not be put on any stage in Czechoslovakia, and then it was not stageable either, but for different reasons. It took the National Theater eighteen months to decide to put it on. This was when it was the fashion to jump to attention at the words "working class." I was one of the few intellectuals who did not wear a worker's peaked cap as a sign of my sympathy with the working class, or my own origins in it. The play itself contained many errors of dramatic structure and other canons; I wrote it in the missionary spirit, for this was the time when in politics and in art the naïve belief reigned that it is enough to present a glowing example in a book or on the stage, and public opinion will obediently follow. However, I did put three real live workers on the stage, credible and complicated characters, of whom one was even a reactionary working-class man. True, I "convinced" him by the end of the play, but that took nothing away from the fact I proved that, even in the working class, you can find many shades of opinion and even reactionary ones.

That was why the play was a success. A wild success.

The greater the stress laid by politicians on the historically progressive role of the working class, its leading role, its all-powerful, all-knowing, all-seeing, and all-resolving role, the harder I tried to show in literature and journalism that this working class was made up of live human beings, who had faults and made mistakes, who were selfish, envious, good, decent, wicked, cynical, greedy, cruel. . . .

In 1955 I published *Marx Street,* a collection of semi-fiction stories, a mixed form, like all I have done in literature to date. There are autobiographical elements in it, but it is really the biography of that one gray, smoke-ridden, working-class street. The book was not a success; it came out in two editions, followed by a Czech and a Hungarian translation, but the critics took little notice of it. There are still people who think it is the best thing I have ever written; I cannot be the judge of that, but it certainly is the book of mine I like best.

I have written hundreds of articles and essays for the press, perhaps as many as a thousand. It took me a long time to get rid of the missionary attitude in my writing, but it would be hard to find a single article in all those years, where I did not take more than the inch allowed by the censor and the Party. The inches became yards. I could take greater and greater liberties, until I was one of the few writers who could take all the liberties he wanted.

I have published twenty books, essays and travel sketches, political studies, a novel and a book of stories, but for the most part I have produced a hybrid literary form which is neither story nor *feuilleton,* neither political essay nor reportage, but a bit of each. After reading the manuscript of my book *Where the Dusty Roads End,* the Party called a meeting to discuss my opinions and actions aimed against it. In order to be present I had to interrupt a period of study abroad, and when I arrived in Bratislava, it was to be told by Šalgovič, who had called the meeting, that it was all a misunderstanding, the book was a very valuable one, based on Marxist ideas and just the thing we needed. It ought to come out in the shortest possible time. A few weeks earlier this same Šalgovič had the forms broken up and threatened the manager of the publishing house concerned that he would be in trouble over it.

This was a collection of studies, almost sociological in character, of out-of-the-way corners of Slovakia; the book appeared, and so a year later did my *Overdue Stories*. This caused a sensation, and sold 300,000 copies in two months, with long lines of people clamoring for more. On the black market the book passed from hand to hand for many times its regular price.

This was again a hybrid literary form, and again a critical approach, this time to the monstrosities of the years of bureaucratic terror. In the West it is supposed to be a bitter denunciation of Socialist justice, but that is only part of the book; it also goes into the results of deformed economic, moral, and human relationships.

I do not think it is a better book than *Dusty Roads;* the latter was less sensational, but I feel that it went deeper.

Whereas I was in danger of expulsion from the Party for *Dusty Roads,* I had no trouble at all over *Overdue Stories*. The first lady of the land is reported to have wondered why the man wasn't in jail, but the book actually came out quickly, smoothly, and without any trouble from the censor.

I hold a curious record for Slovakia: four of my books ended up in "prohibition," as they call the warehouse where books not allowed to be sold or kept in libraries are stored. The subjects are sufficient indication of why: one was about Israel, one about Albania, one about China, and the fourth, a not very good collection of satirical poems, got there by mistake. It was illustrated by one of our best caricaturists, and one of the guardians of the purity of our literary morals thought a certain figure looked like Tito. This was when Tito was no longer a bloodthirsty cur. They feared the caricature, which of course had nothing to do with him at all, might be taken as an insult.

The first of my twenty-odd books to be prohibited before it ever came out was the pamphlet-novel *The Taste of Power*. Now it has appeared in Slovakia, in the summer of 1968. The Czech edition of 160,000 copies is lying ready to be sent out. It is not likely to reach the book counters now. Nor are the Czech and Slovak editions of *The Aggressors,* written in Israel, likely to appear.

I have written only one novel proper, *Death Is Called Engel-*

chen, but even here I was not concerned with fiction. It was discovered later that my book dealt with definite historical events that had taken place at definite places, given their true names in the book, and with actual, nonfictitious people, two of whom, brave and courageous partisan fighters, had been condemned to death by our Socialist courts and executed. By that time it was too late to do anything about the book, which reached a circulation of 300,000 in Czechoslovakia alone.

I was there. At crucial moments of our recent history my pen helped to move things forward, even very early, during the period the West still thinks of as the time "when nothing was happening." My unfinished serial *What Did Not Get into the Papers* was the prelude to the second, stormy Writers' Congress. The short but significant period I spent as chief editor of *Kulturný Život* was the first sounding out of the enemy, between the press and the censorship. At the second Writers' Congress it was my speech, along with those of Seifert and Hrubín, that turned the occasion into a court of judgment on the deformations of our public life. I proposed a general public song and dance in Wenceslas Square, at which half-naked women would dance the cancan and a bonfire be made of the secret files of citizens in the safes of the security police.

It was my article entitled "Conscience" that started off the eventful year 1963, and I was chief editor of *Kulturný Život* in 1964, when the second "Slovak national rising" took place, fighting for the rehabilitation of the real Rising in 1944.

It is impossible to think of Czechoslovak developments without the influence of the paper *Kulturný Život,* which for years was the focal point of intellectual revolt against the dictatorship. I was editor in chief only for short periods, but always at crucial moments.

Then my "flight into Israel" marked the beginning of the end of Novotný's regime.

I must stress again that I was not alone in the struggle; the whole intelligentsia of Czechoslovakia was involved to an ever-increasing degree. Nor was it the intellectuals who actually forced the changes at the end of 1967 and the beginning of

1968; but I was there, and I was proud to be one of the leading rebels.

Enthusiasm was no longer the motive. Nor was naïve faith. Now it was no more than the feeling, the conviction, that someone was waiting to get me by the throat. I did not want to look on while humanity prepared to commit suicide. However hopeless it might be, however inevitable, it was still better to do all you could to turn that fate aside. Better to live in that knowledge than stand by passively waiting for the horror to fall.

My attitude toward the Soviet Union was always sincere. Even sentimental. Up to last year, to the time of the Israel crisis, and then something broke in me. What I had begun to suspect in Vietnam was confirmed by the attitude of all the Socialist countries, except Romania; that attitude of the USSR, and even of Yugoslavia, was a cruel but real fact to be taken into account. The Soviet Union had set out on the path of power politics, the path of expansion, thus deserting the principles on which the victorious revolution of 1917 was founded. In furtherance of "her own interests," the Soviet Union went so far as to support a policy of extermination, the extermination of a complete nation, a small nation.

My discipline went no further. The Soviet Union had saved my little country from extermination by the Nazis and thus laid an obligation on me and on my whole nation. From this obligation she freed me, at least, by her policy toward the remnant of European Jews she had once saved from a terrible death, by her victory over Hitler. Now she had consented to see the little state that emerged twenty years ago as a consequence of her own, Soviet foreign policy, removed from the map.

I was forced to ask myself whether the Soviet Union was playing a straight game. Whether in circumstances where it would suit her she would not desert us, betray us, bargain us away.

What happened was even worse. She occupied our country.

The Seventh Night

On Monday evening we went back into the town. I could not stand being out there, cut off from the world, any longer. In the morning the news bulletin announced the return of Svoboda, Dubček, Smrkovský and Černík from Moscow. One of the radio reporters managed to catch Smrkovský for a few words; he answered in an infinitely tired, sepulchral voice; sad, almost hopeless.

It was terribly hard . . . he said. They had not slept for nights on end. They had all come back, every one of them. That was all the reporter could get out of him. The whole nation was sitting glued to radio receivers, waiting for the President to make his promised speech. Waiting, and waiting, until at last Svoboda spoke. The whole delegation behaved with great courage, he told us, and thanked us for our tireless support. He gave us his word that they had all behaved honorably, and said that they had achieved all that could be achieved. It did not sound promising.

A few hours later Alexander Dubček spoke. He spoke openly, called things by their real name; there were long pauses between his sentences, and twice he seemed to be sobbing. Yet he achieved the impossible: he put new hope into a nation on the verge of despair. He won. The confidence that had been so badly shaken was restored.

What is the good of it? It is in vain. The Soviet authorities cannot leave things at that. They have gone too far to draw back. They are capable of anything, and they cannot be trusted. Their guarantees are no guarantees, their promises no promises; their statement that "as the situation in Czechoslovakia returns to normal we will gradually withdraw our forces" is a tactical move they do not mean even as the words leave their mouths. "Back to normal"—what does that mean? Who is to decide the meaning? What do they mean by it? Something like their idea of "noninterference in the internal affairs of another country"? They cynically declare they are not interfering. The crime of aggression they dignify by the name of fraternal aid. Who can tell what they mean by "back to normal"? At the worst it might mean a Czech or Slovak autonomous republic somewhere between the frontiers of Buryat, Birobidzhan and Yakutsk. They are more likely to give us worse than better.

For the moment the attitude of both the nations of Czechoslovakia is magnificent. But life will not be petrified in this beauty, in a monolithic monument to monolithic unity. The Soviet forces will bore and undermine it, break it down; they will pit one against the other, dictate, provoke. After this one great week there may be others as magnificent, as inspiring— there may be several weeks; but one day something will happen, some trifle in itself, but it will start the crumbling; that will be the first day of the second round.

The consequences are terrible to think of. The finest men any nation had to lead it in this second half of our century carried off to exile from which there is no return. Or shot on the spot, for as long as they remain alive they will be a constant reproach and danger to the Soviet authorities and their puppet government.

They have come back from Moscow, they say it was terribly hard, they call things by their real names, they call for us to maintain our unity, our proud attitude; they declare they have achieved the maximum that could be achieved, that all is not lost.

Nobody expected they would achieve anything more. If the Soviet Government counted on our affection for our leaders changing to anger, that was just another of their miscalculations.

The people love both Svoboda and Dubček, and today more than ever. They realize they could not have acted otherwise and that they cannot act otherwise now, nor will they be able to in the future. Dubček is no mortal now, he is a legend, and that determines his actions. Run away? He cannot run away, that would confirm the Soviet authorities in their mistrust of him— perhaps they are waiting for just that. Dubček will not run away. He must go on as he does until his fate is fulfilled. Years ago Dürenmatt wrote that there is neither pure comedy nor pure tragedy in the world today. He was wrong. Dubček's life is unwinding with the logic of the predetermined fate of a tragic hero of antiquity. With the rape of Czechoslovakia, tragedy regained its pure form. Perhaps years from now, at some Thirtieth Congress of the Communist Party of the Soviet Union, a new Nikita Sergeevich will call the occupation of Czechoslovakia a tragic mistake, and call the culprits to account. There will be another trial of Warren Hastings, brought before an English court by Pitt the Prime Minister, to account for his cruelties during the colonization of India. India got neither freedom nor independence back. It always takes the Great Powers a long time to become ashamed of the shameful things they have done. It always takes them until it is too late to change anything or put anything right. After the war Stalin had the people of the small nations of the Crimea, the Kirghiz and the Chechen, moved en masse to Siberia, on the grounds that they had collaborated with the Nazis. Half of them died on their way to their "new country." Less than twenty years later the Twentieth Congress condemned this act, but did the people get their Crimean home back? It was not only Stalin who was responsible, there were others in it, men who are still alive. Have any of these living lost their important posts? And even if they had, would it have brought back to life those unfortunates who died on the journey or in the inhospitable wastes of Siberia? The only answer one can give is one of Yelochka Shchukinová's eighty words, her famous: ech!

I have always liked the Russians and I still do. It grieves me to think I shall probably never again sit with my friends in

Moscow. I have always been open in my talks with them, although I never expected them to be open with me. And yet a few years ago, in Baku, one of those I liked best confessed: we are a vast country, and man is something very small in it; we are a free great power, but with many nations that are not free.

I like the Russians, and in many ways I think they are a fine people. They are profoundly human, profoundly sad, profoundly unhappy. Those with whom I have made friends in the past are probably profoundly ashamed today. But they will not say so; they will not take any action. They cannot. They know nothing but what others allow them to know. After years of biased information from the radio, television and newspapers, man becomes biased himself. Millions of Soviet citizens are convinced that Czechoslovakia was threatened by counterrevolution, by an anti-Socialist revolution. That is very understandable, for there is nobody even to attempt to suggest the contrary. From reporters of the Zhukov type, they can learn only what Leonid Brezhnev calls the truth.

Many of them, deep inside, have a feeling this is so. It is not a self-assured society; they are afraid. I do not mean just fear of the regime, but a broader fear, turned toward the world outside. They cannot be sure that the world is really like what the servile journalists say it is. Nor can they find out for themselves, for only the elect are allowed to travel abroad.

In Vienna, a few years ago, I met a Moscow friend, a writer I admire for both his work and his personal character. We walked about Vienna, looking in the shop windows. More than half the things we saw there were unknown to him; he did not know what they were or what they were for. He could not read a single label in the Latin alphabet. It was the first time he had been "in the West," and I could see that this first contact with an unknown world was a terrible shock. He cursed capitalism, this degenerate society, the "sweet life" of the bourgeoisie, the West that was out to destroy the Soviet Union. It was sincere enough, the result of the shock at the sight of the vast variety of products which he had never seen in his life and which, if they were to appear in Moscow, would mean lines a mile long. He was comparing it with what he had been told about life on "the other side." The Soviet Union is not to be blamed; she has not yet reached a standard of technical civilization that would allow her people the comfort that is general in the West. But this comfort is in sharp contrast with the way Soviet propaganda praises the superiority of their own products to the skies. The real reason for my friend's outburst of indignation in Vienna was shame at the realization that he had been deceived.

We went to see Pasolini's excellent film *The Gospel of St. Matthew*. For me it was an exhilarating experience, but my friend went out halfway through. Bored. Nothing was happening in the film, and when something did happen he did not understand it. He had never seen the Old or the New Testament, never known the Bible. And he was an excellent Soviet writer, one whose works are translated into many languages.

The occupation of Czechoslovakia will cost the Soviet Union dearly, where they least expect it. Before long the young Soviet soldiers will be coming into contact with the people. They may still think today that the place is full of bourgeois elements, but they will soon see that this is not so. They will see, at least in the limited degree to be found in Czechoslovakia, a level of culture, civilization, and technical progress they have never encountered before. They will sit and talk to young Czechs and Slovaks and hear about things they have never dreamed of before. The invisible army of General Schweik will complete their demoralization. By the time they get home, they will be suffering from schizophrenia. They will talk about what they have seen, heard, learned about. They will spread the disease.

Or else they will be sent to Siberia, like their fathers before them, returning from World War II—sent into quarantine for brainwashing.

I am not ridiculing them, nor being superior; I am not even drawing comparisons. I know how far they have advanced since the Revolution, and I know they could not have got much further. In my varied life I have learned not to draw comparisons, not to measure everything by our foot rule—the worst thing the observer abroad can do.

I cannot agree with those critics of the Soviet Union who ask in surprise: what a state have they brought the Soviet Union to in fifty years of Socialism! They have brought it far indeed, though not as far as Socialism could have come. The fifty years, these critics forget, were no idyllic years of gentle growth. After the Revolution the country began from naught, technically speaking. They built up their Soviet state surrounded by hostile countries, and then bore the main burden of the iron attack of Fascism. They had to feed its steel jaws with human flesh to make up at least to some degree for the technical superiority of the enemy. Their losses were enormous; after the war there was hardly a family in the Soviet Union that did not have a loss to weep for. In the first postwar years, the whole burden of reconstruction lay on the shoulders of the women, for there were hardly any men left. Tightening their belts, they built up again from the ground much of what they had already built that way once, only to have it destroyed by the war. And they had to drive the country forward in one direction, to catch up with the United States and break the atom bomb monopoly.

Those are bare facts. But somewhere along the line, it began to turn their heads. They may have got tired of trying to solve the insoluble problems of their own society. Expansion is always a sign of something wrong within; a show of force is always a cover for internal lability and weakness. The administrative system of the Soviet Union cannot cope with the problems of the day, and so her leaders decided to turn the people's attention elsewhere—to an external show of force, to a new wave of anti-Semitism inside the country. That is always a sign of crisis within a society. They decided for expansion, and that is something a Socialist state cannot do and remain Socialist. Nowhere in Marx or in Lenin can they find justification for the occupation of Czechoslovakia. It is their "original" contribution to the development of this ideology, in contradiction of the eternal truth enshrined in Marx's comment that no nation can be free that destroys the freedom of another nation.

There are many to comment on and explain the first open expansive campaign by the Soviet Union. That it is the outcome of profound internal crisis. That it was called for by Ulbricht and Gomulka, who feared that the liberalization of Czechoslovakia would have repercussions in their own countries. That is a false assumption. These countries, including the Soviet Union herself, would have more to fear from the demoralizing influence of occupied Czechoslovakia. Just as the Soviet leaders managed to hide from their own people the true motives of their aggression, so they would be able to hide from them the true state of democracy we had attained. In East Germany neither Ulbricht nor the people have any say in the matter; it is absurd to imagine that the Soviet Union would bother about Ulbricht's fears for his Prussian-Saxon Socialism. Gomulka has already worked out his conflict with liberal tendencies. In Hungary things are developing in their own way, tolerated by the Soviet Union.

It is unthinkable that the Soviet marshals would not have realized the true distribution of power in Europe. The claims of Soviet propaganda that Czechoslovakia was menaced by West German revanchism is an invention they do not believe themselves. But if the occupation of Czechoslovakia was not a defensive move to protect Socialism, which was not threatened either within the country or from without, what is the alternative explanation?

The alternative explanation is expansion. Expansion into Europe.

And they could not have thought of carrying out this expansion unless there were other conditions, outside Europe, of which we know nothing as yet.

I fear that there is a dirty bargain behind it. Vietnam in exchange for Czechoslovakia. The Soviet has made no answer to this suggestion; the Americans have vaguely denied it. Johnson talks about the inviolability of West Berlin, but not about the inviolability of West Germany, which he logically should. Yet it is clear to all that the occupation of Czechoslovakia has changed the strategic situation in Europe; the offensive and defensive conception of NATO is now worthless. If the United States decides to leave ungrateful Europe to its own devices, there is no power capable of standing up to the Soviet Union in either the military or the political sphere. That U.S. Secretary of State Dean Rusk should be surprised at West Germany's Chancellor Kurt Kiesinger asking for a special meeting of NATO was more than suspicious. This meeting would have been the first consequence of the Soviet steps, the first reaction of the West— regardless of whether Czechoslovakia was free or not, for that is a trifle in global strategy. That the Americans not only did not ask for the meeting, but even torpedoed it, suggests that in the near future the world will be presented with something particularly nasty—a new Yalta, a new division of spheres of interest by the two greatest powers.

The security of the United States does not depend on the security of Europe today, in these days of nuclear warfare. Today the Soviet Union can be attacked from the bottom of the sea, and so can the United States. Why bother so much about Europe? If there is any threat to the two powers, it is from the vast territory of China. Shortly before the occupation of Czechoslovakia, the two powers signed a blackmailing agreement against passing on atomic weapons to any third power. That is an open threat to China. Leaving aside the power politics of China, which are no better than any other, let us look at the immorality of this agreement. We have them, but let nobody else try to have them! Is this not a clear sign of increasing inequality, a debasement of the sovereignty of all other nations?

Somewhere in the background there is China. The Americans fear the "export of revolution"; the Soviet Union feels directly threatened. She has a common frontier with China stretching for thousands of miles, and Mao has declared China's right to usurp Soviet territory.

Is that the only combination possible? One thing is sure— whoever gets China on her side will be the stronger and will have the advantage over the other. They will no longer be equal.

The United States and the Soviet Union may have come to some agreement on how to meet the common Chinese threat. But it is possible that the United States may come to terms with China against the Soviet Union, and there is a third alternative: the renewal of the broken relationship between the two biggest countries in the world, the two Socialist Great Powers. The Molotov-Ribbentrop Pact can be repeated, anytime. Each of the three powers is cynical enough to see nothing in the way of such an advantageous step. And it is not likely that the idea has never occurred to them.

I was against the enslavement of the world by capitalist imperialism. But I am also decidedly against the enslavement of the world by Socialist imperialism. The use of force is anti-Marxist, anti-Socialist, in whatever form. The position of Socialism cannot be defended the way the imperialists try to gain world domination. Socialism and the victory of Socialism anywhere in the world is a question for every nation to decide for itself. It cannot be exported in tanks and bayonets; that is against its very nature. Brezhnev the Leninist should know that better than anyone else.

I am against war, against occupation, against any form of national, racial, or class oppression. That is what my Communist convictions, and not only mine, tell me. That is why, the main reason why, I became a Communist.

As far as I am aware, Marx and Lenin were against these things, too; in fact Lenin carried his convictions into practice. If Leonid Brezhnev considers these maxims of Lenin on which the whole of Socialist ideology is based to be out of date and useless, he should say so; let him explain the occupation of Czechoslovakia not by a lie, which is proverbially short-winded, but by an analysis of the political theory. I am willing to learn and to act accordingly. A certain Napoleon once abused and destroyed the great idea of revolution. Does Brezhnev see himself as a new Napoleon, a Red Napoleon? Let him not commit an error. But if the time is in any way ripe for a Red Napoleon, then Brezhnev is cast for the role of Barras. History will call his "time" an unworthy Directoire.

I walked through the evening streets asking myself: where was it? Where did we make our mistake? Where, when did it happen? At Munich? In 1945? In 1948? In 1956? Or in 1968? I had to laugh at myself. How naïve and blind we were, we Communists and all those who came along with us. Those we attacked saw further than we did. How many militant articles in defense of the Soviet Union have I not written against them—you there, on the dung heap of history, you forgers of history and distorters of the truth, what are you doing on the face of the earth? Why haven't you crept back into your holes? But it was they who saw clearly while we were blind and deaf in the face of cold reality. Not that they were right—they were equally blinded, seeing only our faults while we saw only theirs.

Would it have been any good if we had seen clearly? Maybe. Maybe in 1948 it would still have helped. Czechoslovakia could still have taken a more independent stand. Tito managed to do so, at least for twenty years. And there is no doubt that if the Soviet Union attempts to invade Yugoslavia, Tito will fight. The Russians will be able to destroy Yugoslav independence only by a war, not by an invasion with no opposition.

What the Soviet Union has done to us was not such a shock and surprise, but what about the hundreds of thousands of Czechoslovak Communists who trusted Soviet policy right up to the last moment? What do they feel about it now? We Communists always had the worst of it. The hostile world did not trust us and our own treated us like dirt. What does Brezhnev care for the feelings of nearly two million Czechoslovak Communists? And the feelings of millions of Communists elsewhere in Europe?

I walked about the city, fully lighted in the evening, but empty. There were few tanks in the streets and squares of Bratislava that seventh night. They had retired to the outskirts. I did not go near those that were still parked at important spots; I could see them from far off and make a detour around them. When I heard the sound of a car, I hid in the nearest doorway. It could only be a Soviet armored car on patrol. Not a single private car passed through the streets of Bratislava that night.

The people were few and far between. Here and there they spoke in low tones in front of their houses, probably wondering what was going to happen. As I passed they looked at me suspiciously. The old mood is back again, everyone is suspicious of his fellows.

The Russians are here. They won't be going away. It would

be foolish to hope they will. Here they are and here they stay. They may be driven out by the next war, but the next war would mean the end of this country, the end of this nation. The presence of the Russians has made Czechoslovakia one of the most important strategic areas, on which the interest and the rockets of our potential future enemy will be focused. The occupation has made Czechoslovakia into a dangerous wedge thrust into the security system of Western Europe. The strategists of the West will change their defensive and offensive plans accordingly. In these, Czechoslovakia will become the point for the first aggressive or retaliatory blow.

Walking about during the day, I met people I knew. Some of them pretended not to see me. Others looked at me in horror. What are you doing here? Why haven't you disappeared? Quick, get away while there's still time—every hour may be the last. Others stared as though I were a ghost, a corpse, a man with the sign of leprosy. They had written me off. Actually it was time that had written me off. There was no place in the country safe for me, no scrap of hope. Whatever illusions I tried to cherish, the eyes of my friends, especially those who care for me, spoke clearly. There is no need, I'll go. I only wanted to see the end, feel it, live through it.

I walked about the dead night city, and it was the seventh night. How very much alive the city used to be! Music came from the dance bands into the half-lighted streets; gay youngsters woke the sleepers with their singing and shouting. Cars slid over the asphalt roads, coming from the unknown, into the unknown. The squeals of young girls, laughter, anger, lightheartedness, sorrow, the smell of gasoline, of hamburgers, neon lights, the starry sky, the unsteady footsteps of a drunk, the monumental calm of great buildings, light and darkness, quiet and noise, longing and hopelessness, love and nostalgia, the strange melancholy that falls on big cities at night, here and there a window lighted in expectation or restlessness; the majestic calm of all those windows where the sleepers lay. Crime crept along the dark street and an ambulance siren wailed in the distance. The disturbing tapping of a young woman's heels, hurrying perhaps from her lover, perhaps to her lover . . . how often had I thought out those thousands of lives behind drawn blinds—a petrified city, turned to stone at one touch, and only I am alive, only I walk the streets and gaze around, seeing what no one will ever see again: a young man caressing a young woman in bed, a young man strangling an old, sick woman, a scientist at a rococo desk calculating in complicated equations, all the sorrows and sins and hopes of the night; I wanted to see them all, live through them all. I walked along behind the man with the strange job of shooting pigeons, reducing their numbers to keep down the damage they did to the roofs of the old buildings, and who carried out this task, to save the sensitive feelings of the city fathers, in that unidentifiable hour between night and morning, when so many, so very many people were asleep. Gas lamps . . . there are still a few in the old part of the city; an old woman goes around at night to light them with a long rod, but I have never been able to catch her putting them out in the morning. The well-known silhouette of familiar buildings, twisted, shabby; quiet courtyards, sleeping bars smelling of stale beer, wine cellars where I have spent so many night hours, a police patrol in wait around a dark corner, the lighted windows of the hospital emergency ward, a deserted gasoline pump . . .

This night it was different, everything shouted differently, everything was different in its quiet, different in its melancholy. . . .

The shop windows were plastered with posters and slogans, there were slogans painted across the house fronts; at a corner of the street a little altar covered with fresh flowers and a name written in crooked letters on a piece of cardboard, the name of a seventeen-year-old girl, shot by a twenty-year-old soldier perhaps from Siberia, perhaps a slant-eyed Kalmuck. The dark, dead windows of *Kulturný Život* . . . they open and I hear twenty hoarse voices singing and shouting . . . somebody calls out to me, "Hi there, Laco, come on in." But I shake my head. No, I'm not coming in, I'll never be in there again, I'm saying good-bye, it was good being with you, we had some good times even in those dark, stifling years. . . . The house I lived in, lived in but won't be living in anymore, the devil take all the belongings in there; no, I'm not going in, I'll go away as I am, travel light, that's the way, all that stuff up there, the bed with the familiar hollow in the mattress, the pictures on the walls, and the books—all those books! That is all past and gone, there is nothing of it left in this strange night, nothing but an aria from the "The Jacobites" running around in my head, farewell, farewell my city, I loved you; you were my great living room, my bedroom, my dining room, my drawing room, my home, but the Russians have come and you are my home no longer, I don't want you anymore, you would get in my way; even so, you still are there, the one heavy, heavy burden one can never throw off, never hand on; nobody has ever got rid of you when he left for the place I'm going to. . . . You used to be gay, now you will be sad; you used to be loved, now you are cursed; you used to be loving, now you are cruel; you used to be my refuge, now you are a trap; you used to be mine, now you are mine no longer. . . .

For ten months you were forbidden to me, but I used to fly overhead, not too high up, not too far off; as the plane came down on the Vienna airfield, I looked at you from the cabin window and saw your roofs and the shapes of your buildings; more than once I felt like jumping out, or shouting something loud enough for you to hear—and I wasn't an *émigré,* I replied to everyone everywhere, every time: I haven't emigrated, I'm going back there, soon, soon now. . . .

I came back, only to leave again forever. I have not gone yet, I am still treading your pavements, but I am an *émigré,* I am already an *émigré;* I fear the word, I fear the life, I fear the melancholy, but the Russians are here, the Russians are here and you are no longer the same city and you never will be the same again for me.

A long, long time ago, before Cromwell and before Luther, long before Robespierre, a revolution flared up in this land. A great revolution, purifying, terrifying, terrible, the first revolution in Europe, the first revolution in Europe against the Church of Rome, against the feudal castles, against poverty. The cruel continent sent army after army against the rebels, in vain; the armored infantry, those tanks of the Middle Ages, turned and fled in fear at the mere sound of the rebels' hymns. It took the cruel continent two hundred years to put them down, to disperse them, to do away with that revolution altogether.

The cruel emperor pressed the remnants of the Czech Brethren, the spiritual elite of the continent, to return; come back to the bosom of the true Church, come back, oh, you who have strayed, come back and you will live and be free and respected, in your own homes. They did not come back; they left their homes and dispersed to all corners of the world to teach the truth, preach the truth, speak the truth. As they crossed the borders of their homeland, they bent to kiss the earth, took up a handful for remembrance, wept, and sang their melancholy lament:

"Nothing did we take with us but the Word,
  The Kralice Bible and the Labyrinth of the World . . ."

So has departed the intellectual flower of the small, ravished, humiliated nation, and I want to shout after them: brothers, do not go! I must, I have no other choice, but you need not, you can stay—stay with your broken, humiliated people!

It is a vain call. The third wave of destruction is pouring over the Communist intelligentsia. The third in one generation. Will they go away? Then they will be lost like grains of sand in the desert; if they do not go they will be attacked, terrified, crushed, destroyed.

It was simply too good to be true. Too good . . . and too human. Oh, my country, with your mountains and plains, your forests and cliffs, how often the hooves of foreign horses have trampled you, how often tracks of foreign tanks have crushed you. The Germans moved along your rivers, the Avaric Huns slashed you with their whips, Hungarians, Poles, more Germans, Swedes, Frenchmen, more Germans . . . what had you done to them? What evil had you done to anyone? When had you made war against others, when had you enslaved other peoples, what was the curse on you, why did they hate you? There was always someone there to liberate you from your freedom, to protect you from others. You have been Germanized, Magyarized, they tried to make you Polish, and now the Russians have come. . . .

I sat on a bench in the little park where the bronze statue of Stalin once stood. Well, Joseph Vissarionovich, what is the taste of immortality like? They took you down, shamed you, threw you out of the mausoleum for having been so cruel, so wicked, for having trampled the law underfoot, for following your own goal, looking neither to right nor left. The halo of your immortality faded before ten years was out; they threw all manner of crimes at your head, including their own, and swore never to let anything like that happen again. They called that period after you, the Stalin era, the cult of the personality. . . .

He was not there on his pedestal anymore, but I thought I could hear his sarcastic laugh ringing out over the city, over the country, over the almost endless continent. On the pedestal someone had scrawled with a piece of chalk: Workers of the world unite, or I shoot!

Next morning, after that seventh night, I was seized by panic. I got into a taxi.

"To the Austrian border . . ."

I thought he would refuse, but he took me there. He did not say a word the whole way. . . .

Somewhere in Austria, September 1–20, 1968